HERITAGE WALKS AROUND VANCOUVER

HERITAGE WALKS AROUND VANCOUVER

MICHAEL KLUCKNER
and
JOHN ATKIN

WHITECAP BOOKS
Vancouver/Toronto

Copyright © 1992 by Michael Kluckner and John Atkin
Whitecap Books
Vancouver/Toronto

Edited by Elaine Jones
Cover design by Warren Clark
Interior design by Susan Doering
Typography by CryptoGraphics, Vancouver, B.C., Canada

Printed and bound in Canada.

Canadian Cataloguing in Publication Data

Kluckner, Michael.
    Heritage walks around Vancouver

    Includes index.
    ISBN 1-55110-036-3

    1. Walking—British Columbia—Vancouver—Guidebooks.
2. Vancouver (B.C.)—Tours. 3. Historic buildings
—British Columbia—Vancouver. I. Atkin, John, 1957-
II. Title.
FC3847.7.K68 1992   917.11'33   C92-091527-2
F1089.5.V22K68 1992

To the Y and M Show — *M.K.*

For my Dad — *J.A.*

Contents

Preface

Preface

This set of eight tours evolved over the past few years because of our efforts to encourage heritage preservation, initially with the Community Arts Council of Vancouver and more recently with the Heritage Vancouver Society. We feel that the will to preserve buildings and neighbourhoods grows from an appreciation of their value, both as historical and as modern communities. These tours provide some historical and architectural background to encourage that appreciation. Besides, walking through neighbourhoods and looking at buildings and gardens is one of the great joys of city life.

It is easy to become so enchanted with architectural quality and detailing that you search only for the buildings that are the gems of a neighbourhood; likewise, historical anecdote can be quaint and fun, and can easily become an end in itself. It is better to combine the appreciation of architecture and history with a recognition of how modern lifestyles can adapt to old neighbourhoods, and how old neighbourhoods can continue to function in massive modern cities, and thus to understand the real issues of heritage preservation. We have written these tours to reflect our concern not only with the past, but with the present and the future.

The terminology for architectural detailing and styles can become arcane but, like other languages such as Computer-Speak, it is a convenient and descriptive shorthand that is worth learning. The glossary at the back of the book will eliminate the need to carry a large dictionary.

John Atkin wrote the Strathcona and Coffee Shop tours; Michael Kluckner wrote the Nelson Park, Delamont Park, Kitsilano and Kerrisdale tours; we jointly researched the Grandview and North Vancouver tours. John Atkin drew the maps and we both took photographs; credits for the historical photographs are printed along with the captions.

M.K. and J.A.
June, 1992

Strathcona

1 ½ HOURS

T he City of Vancouver had its birth at the foot of Dunlevy Avenue, two blocks to the east of Main Street, on a spit of land where, in 1865, Captain Edward Stamp tried for a second time to establish a sawmill on Burrard Inlet. His first attempt, in what is now Stanley Park near Lumbermen's Arch, failed because the strong First Narrows currents threatened to sweep away both ships and wharfs. To supply the new mill, he negotiated a lease on over twenty thousand acres of forest, four thousand of which were held under a crown lease, for fifteen cents an acre per annum. The mill was not a success for Stamp, but survived and thrived under new owners. By 1873, the Hastings Mill grounds had on its six acres a store, a mess house, a kitchen, housing for mill workers and a school.

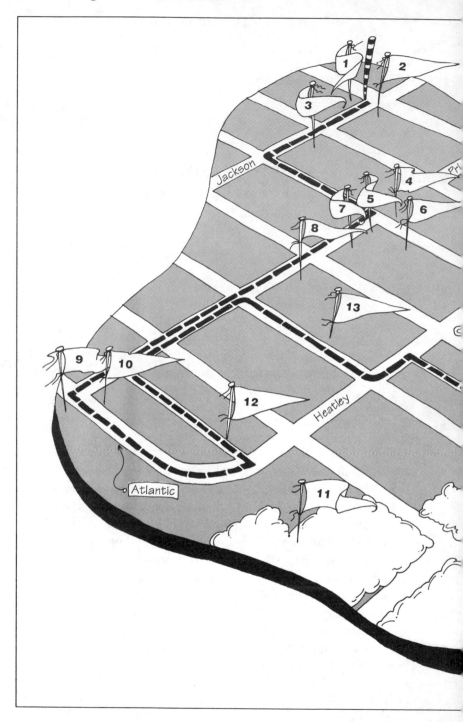

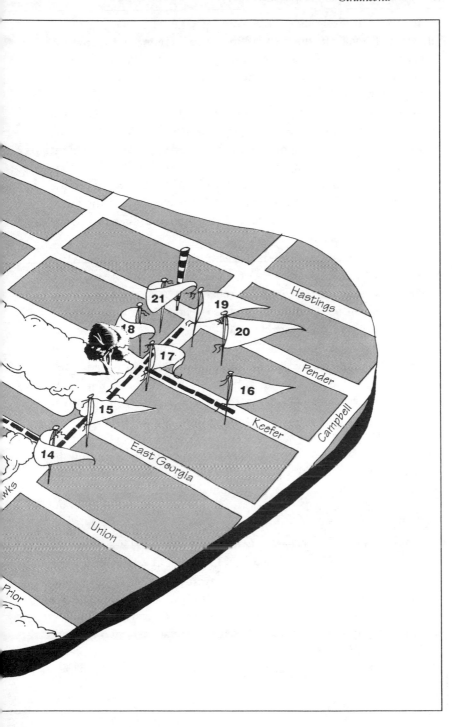

Just outside the grounds, the town of Granville sprang up with saloons and hotels. In the early 1880s, as vast crews constructed the Canadian Pacific Railway westward towards the Pacific Ocean, rumours about where the terminus would be established increased land speculation in the area.

By the time of the railway's arrival, the owners of the Hastings Mill had sold most of their crown lease to the Oppenheimer Brothers, David and Isaac, who operated as the Vancouver Improvement Company. Under the laws of the time, a crown lease could be converted to freehold if the land was purchased at $2.50 an acre, which the Improvement Company did, so that by 1889 it was listed as the third-largest landowner, after the CPR and the mill, and effectively controlled the eastern half of the new city.

The Oppenheimers cleared three hundred acres between Main Street and Clark Drive and began to offer lots for sale; as well, they erected houses on lots selected by purchasers, which could be bought on an instalment plan with a term of ten years. Prices were $350 to $800 per lot, with the average being $500.

In 1887, the Hastings Mill School was demolished because it sat on the CPR right-of-way. Its eight-room replacement opened at the corner of Jackson and Cordova with an enrolment of 285 pupils. As population grew in the new city, more schools were planned, so that by 1891 there were the Central and High schools just south of Victory Square, the West End School, the Mount Pleasant School at Kingsway and Broadway, as well as a new East End School. Built to the design of Thomas Hooper on the highest point of land in the neighbourhood, the corner of Jackson and Pender, East End School was renamed for Lord Strathcona, president of the CPR. It is from the school that "the neighbourhood of the lumberman and the mechanic," as the 1891 *William's Directory* described it, took its name.

As you walk through Strathcona, you can see the scars left by the various government policies and actions—intended to improve and renew the neighbourhood—that were tried out in the 1950s and 1960s. But more importantly you can see what has survived: houses, some of this city's earliest, standing next to lots that have two or more buildings on them. A development pattern that grew out of the actions of individual property owners, without the "benefit" of modern planning or zoning ideas, has given us a neighbourhood of homes, rooming houses, apartment buildings, and grocery stores. As you will see, this can lead to many interesting juxtapositions that are not found anywhere else in the city, a situation that zoning or planning probably could not re-create no matter how hard they tried.

Start at the corner of East Hastings and Jackson.

From the corner of Hastings and Jackson, you can see the contrasts between, on the west side of Jackson, the simple frame house high above the traffic **(1)** and on the east, the faded grandeur of Ferrera Court **(2)**, clearly demonstrating the unplanned nature of this neighbourhood and the different opinions people held about its potential. The former was built before 1890 by A.F. Bradley, when Hastings was a residential street and Main Street at Hastings was considered, as city archivist Major J.S. Matthews recollected, to be "too far from the business section [Cordova Street] to be successful." Today, the little house sits isolated high above the street on what was the original forest floor, and appears never to have been painted since its construction and original coat of red paint.

Compare this with the imposing Ferrera Court, which was built in

1. *The Bradley house at the southwest corner of Hastings and Jackson.*

2. Ferrera Court under construction in 1912. (Photographer unknown, VPL 7450)

1912 by Cavaliere Agostino Gabriele Ferrera, the Italian consul of Vancouver, a Knight of the Crown of Italy and a restaurateur. Conceived as a gracious apartment building that would take advantage of the streetcar line and the eastward expansion of the city, it was obviously the right building at the wrong time. Like the little Bradley house across the street, Ferrera Court has suffered the ravages of time, losing its ornate cornice decorated with lions' heads. Nevertheless, it retains a minor claim to fame: it was here while visiting friends with Zeppo Marx that Jack Benny met his future wife, Mary Livingstone. She was twelve at the time and "didn't like actors," according to an interview she gave in the forties; they later met again in Chicago and were married. Jack Benny claimed he couldn't remember their first meeting.

Walk south on Jackson to Pender, then continue one block to Keefer.

At the corner of Jackson and Pender is Strathcona School. When the 1891 building (now demolished) was erected, it was the major building on the east side of the city, its tower being visible from across both False Creek and Burrard Inlet. As the community grew, a second school was built, the impressive brick structure facing Keefer Street one block south of Pender. Designed by William Blackmore in 1897, it is the oldest school building still standing in Vancouver. In the decades since, it has lost its tower roof and the entrance on Keefer is no longer used.

The third addition to Strathcona School is the Senior Building facing Jackson Street (3). It was designed on a sixteen-room plan and in 1915 the first eight rooms were opened to great fanfare; the *Daily News Advertiser* called it "one of the finest buildings of its kind on the Pacific Coast." In response to increasing enrolment, the southern half of the building was constructed in 1929.

At the rear of the Senior Building, a large, painted-glass window in the central stairwell features an ornate early city crest and medallion portraits of Burns, Moore and Shakespeare. The window was designed and constructed by the craftsman Clifford Mason, whose family lived at 851 Union Street, and whose father, James, had started the Terminal City Iron Works. Clifford Mason had apprenticed with the Standard Glass Company, run by Charles Bloomfield. Charles, his brother James, and his father Henry were considered some of the best glass artists in British Columbia; the Bloomfields are responsible for,

3. *Looking southeast in 1915 from the corner of Jackson and Pender at the first, eight-room section of the Senior Building of Strathcona School; the 1891 Thomas Hooper-designed school, demolished in the 1920s, stands to its left. Note that the old school stands at the original road height.* (Dominion Photo Company, VPL 20389)

among other things, the windows in the Parliament Buildings in Victoria and the hallway leadlight at "Gabriola," now the Mansion Restaurant on Davie Street. Mason also produced the heraldic windows in the great hall of the UBC Library. (The Senior Building window may be difficult to see because the courtyard has had large chain-link gates installed to keep the increasing population of prostitutes and drug pushers from using the courtyard after school hours.)

As the Senior Building was being completed, the 1891 building was being demolished; the bricks were used to build the nicely proportioned Primary School, designed by F.A.A. Barrs in 1921, on the Pender Street side of the complex. In the 1970s, the construction of the community centre entailed the closing of Princess Street, causing the demolition of the turn-of-the-century East End Grocery, later

4. *The Strathcona Grocery, which stood at Princess and Keefer until the 1970s.*
(Photographer unknown c. 1960, collection John Atkin)

known as the Strathcona Grocery **(4)**, and the block of houses adjoining it .

By 1890, most of the development around the school site had taken place in the blocks to the northwest of Jackson. Other houses were built soon thereafter along Pender Street eastward to Campbell Avenue to be near the interurban line which ran along Hastings, then turned onto Campbell before heading off into the wilds of what is now Grandview-Woodlands.

Walk east on Keefer to Princess, then walk south on Princess.

At the corner of Princess and Keefer stands the home built for the first principal of Strathcona School, Gregory Tom **(5)**. Prior to moving to this home, Tom lived at 316 Union Street. His new house, built in 1900, takes advantage of its corner site with a central entrance and turret from which, according to school lore, he supervised the school grounds. The two gable ends have the original decorative fretwork. After many years, during which the house was unsympathetically renovated, the front porch has been reopened to

5. The 1900 Tom house at 602 Keefer.

reveal the original stained-glass windows on either side of the front door, as part of a careful and authentic restoration.

Across the street at 603-621 Princess, the builder William H. Rogers purchased two twenty-five-foot lots in 1907 and built on them four substantial homes, which he then rented out at a substantial profit. Rogers was responding to a property boom that had begun in Vancouver in the late 1890s and continued until just before the First World War. In this booming market, building lots were purchased by everyone: shop clerks, factory men and mill workers, along with accountants and businessmen—a cross-section of the city's population. When the boom ended, some lost everything, while others managed to make ends meet and survive with their holdings intact until the economy finally rebounded in the 1920s; some just left and went to war.

Gregory Tom's house and the houses built by William Rogers represent the second phase of development in Strathcona. In the 1880s there had been some small homes built along the newly surveyed streets. As the area developed, these modest buildings were demolished for bigger, grander homes, an example of which is two doors down from principal Tom's house at 620 Keefer **(6)**. It is a large house that sits across two lots and was built in 1895 by J.G. Vickers, who worked for Royal City Planing Mills and had been living on Pender Street. His house apparently replaced an earlier 1880s cottage occupied by Mr. Hall, a partner in Hall and Beatty, greengrocers and produce merchants eight blocks away at 140 Cordova Street. The Vickers house is one of the best preserved in the neighbourhood and, because of its larger lot, has two bay windows instead of the usual one; as well, it has a prominent gable with fretwork in the peak. The asphalt shingles imitating stone cladding were added as an "improvement" to the sides of the house many years after it was built. It is worth walking up the lane, not only to see the garden but also to see the original condition of the rear of the house.

Back on Princess Street, the house behind Tom's, at 616 Princess, was built in 1902 by the McNair family. Three of the family members were teachers: Clara taught at the Dawson School in the West End, Muriel at Grandview School and Miss L.S. McNair at Strathcona. Curiously, the water permit signed by Agnes McNair in 1902 lists the property use as a Chinese rooming house.

6. The 1895 Vickers house at 620 Keefer.

Just to the south of the McNair house at 630 Princess, on the edge of the lane, is a house which shares the lot with its neighbour to the south **(7)**. Number 630 Princess was built in the Queen Anne style in 1898 and has the characteristic large, ornate brackets at the gables and porch. The front and side bay windows have the original coloured-glass insets surrounding the central pane; these often do not survive renovations and in many other houses in Strathcona have been replaced with ribbed or plain glass. The wonderful paint job on this house is neither original nor authentic—nor is it an attempt at copying the San Francisco idea of house painting—it is just a pure expression of colour. In 1908 Robert Percy, Master Mariner, lived here. Strathcona was home to many early captains and master mariners, engineers and other ships' hands. Most of these men rented their homes, and some lived in three or four houses in as many years.

At the corner of Georgia and Princess are daycare facilities of St.

7. The 1898 Queen Anne at 630 Princess.

Frances Xavier—a major presence in the neighbourhood with a church and elementary school among other services. Although built in the 1980s, this building is, despite its concrete walls and sheet-metal roof, a very pleasant structure that manages to fit into the fabric of the neighbourhood.

Across the street, tucked in behind 700 Princess, is a small one-room house that was built before the larger home at the front of the lot was constructed in 1898 **(8)**. It was more usual in this neighbourhood for the smaller house to be knocked down after the new house was completed.

A few steps away, at Union and Princess, is Benny's Italian Market. Benny's opened in 1912 as a grocery store and ice-cream parlour. While ice cream is no longer served, the original marble-topped counter is still there.

Union Street has some of the earliest homes in Strathcona. The

8. Early-1890s cottage behind 700 Princess Street.

north side of the street was almost completely built up by 1895, at least as far as Heatley, and the majority of the homes were built by 1892. In 1895, you could meet, in the 500-block of Union, William Paddon, the engineer on the Imperial Timber and Trading Company's steam-tug *Saturna*; or the four Langdale brothers, who were respectively a rancher, a butcher, a painter and a printer; or Airne Pare, who was an architect. In 1898, Robert Lundy lived on the block in between voyages aboard the *Empress of India*.

Continue on Princess Street across Prior Street to Atlantic; walk east on Atlantic to Heatley.

At the corner of Princess and Atlantic you can stand on a bluff and overlook the roof of a warehouse, the railyards, and Mount Pleasant in the distance. It takes a bit of imagination to see water instead of trains here, yet prior to 1915 False Creek extended all the way up to Clark Drive and over to the shore of Mount Pleasant, from where early ranchers and settlers often rowed into town for provisions **(9)**.

In the early days of the city, the low land along Campbell Avenue provided a tidal and wet-weather "canoe route" between Burrard

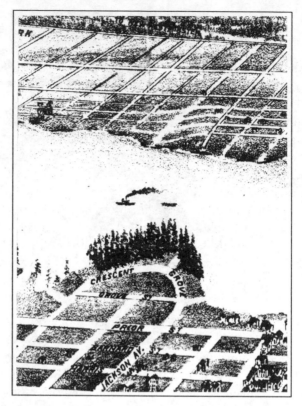

9. *A bird's-eye view published in the* World *newspaper in 1890, looking south over Strathcona to the False Creek mudflats.* (Collection John Atkin)

Inlet and False Creek, creating the possibility of the latter becoming a port for deep-sea ships and coastal shipping. The City Engineer prepared plans in December, 1905, for an excavated False Creek channel east of Main Street, docks, a channel connecting to Burrard Inlet, and a bascule-span bridge at Main Street to replace the 1872 trestle that crossed False Creek there. However, the Great Northern Railway approached the city in 1909 with plans to use the upper creek for its rail terminal. An eventual agreement granted the GNR 61 acres in a horseshoe shape around the edges of the creek. The possibility of a port within this development remained until the forerunner of Canadian National Railways, Canadian Northern Pacific, applied to the city for the remaining 160 acres of the upper creek. The GNR had agreed to erect a passenger terminal and other facilities at a cost of no less than $2.5 million on its portion of the reclamation, and the CNPR offered to erect two hotels, one on its reclaimed land and the other downtown (today's Hotel Vancouver is the result). As well, the CNPR agreed to provide deep-water wharves and even start up a steamship line. The filling of the creek was finished by 1918.

Before the railway companies filled the creek, the streets along the Strathcona side were called Grove Street and Grove Crescent after a stand of trees at the edge of the point. Grove Crescent and the homes that lined it disappeared when Malkin Street was constructed (south of Prior Street) and the point was chopped away during the filling of the creek. Later, the name Grove was changed to Bayview, even though any view of water had long since disappeared, and eventually became the equally pointless Atlantic **(10)**. Some accounts of early Vancouver history claim that Grove and the Crescent were "exclusive" streets, but directory information and early photographs indicate that these blocks were just like the rest of the neighbourhood. Some residents did give their homes special treatment—one house had very elaborate painted and hand-stencilled decorations on the walls and ceilings of all the main rooms instead of the usual

10. Houses on Atlantic Street, dating from the turn of the century.

11. Looking north over the vegetable plots at the Strathcona Community Garden.

wallpaper. Some of the decorations were just hand-rendered versions of wallpaper borders, but others showed overflowing cornucopias filled with fruits and vegetables and hand-painted representations of plaster mouldings.

During the Depression, the Great Northern Railway was unable to pay its taxes on the "flats" and the city, in lieu of monies owed, took possession of what is today Strathcona Park and the Strathcona Community Garden. The community garden, behind the fire hall, sits on a site that was once part of the city dump and was home in the 1930s to a shanty town accommodating a few hundred transient, unemployed men. Despite being a designated park, the site spent many years as a wasteland until residents in the community lobbied to obtain a lease on the land to build a garden. Today, after many years of hard work and the removal of an amazing collection of junk, this three-acre site provides neighbourhood people with vegetable plots, an apple orchard, a herb garden and a wildlife area, where native species of plants and trees are grown **(11)**.

Walk north on Heatley to the lane between Atlantic and Prior, then walk west along the lane to Princess.

12. Former cow barn in the lane between Prior and Atlantic.

After the creek was filled, area residents grazed their cattle on the land not used by the trains (a 1902 by-law limited the number of cows within the city limits to twenty-five per household). These cows were kept in small barns in the lanes of the neighbourhood, and the lane between Prior and Atlantic, known to local children as "cowshit alley," still has a couple of barns on it. Other lanes in Strathcona also have small horse and cow barns, though most are now used for cars—look for large, top-hung sliding doors and a hayloft door on the upper level; sometimes the hook for hauling up hay bales is still there **(12)**.

Walk north on Princess to Union, turn east (right) and walk to Heatley Avenue; at Heatley turn left, then right into the lane between Union and Georgia, and walk to Hawks Avenue.

In this block of Union you can see how much the topography of the neighbourhood has changed. The houses have ended up at least twelve feet above the street level due to the program of street leveling started in the 1890s **(13)**. On the south side of the street, 624 Union was the home of A.D. Ford, who worked for the City Tramway Company. Built in 1892, it is a good example of a modest home of the period that, apart from some decorative porch brackets, was built

13. The north side of Union east of Princess Street.

without the elaborate (and quite expensive) fretwork decoration found elsewhere. The house has no basement and, in fact, if you were able to pick it up off its foundation you would more than likely find tree needles, branches, a reddish-brown soil and in some cases tree trunks, because most of the early homes were built directly on the cleared forest floor, with concrete blocks on the four corners for a foundation.

Farther along Union lived more of Strathcona's early seafarers. Number 651 was home in 1895 to Captain E.C. Bridgeman, and four years later to Captain Edward Hastings. Captain James Woodworth lived at 657 Union in 1899.

The gradual erosion of the original streetscapes by the intrusion of the "Vancouver Special" is particularly noticeable here on the north side of Union just before Heatley. Note also the "Joe Wai Specials" designed by the architect Joe Wai, at the northeast corner of Heatley and Union. Built in the 1970s, after the folly of urban renewal was abandoned, in an attempt to provide affordable housing and a sympathetic design in new construction, these homes are dotted throughout the neighbourhood and occupy former vacant lots.

Looking down Union at this point, you can see how much the street-leveling program changed the topography. The north side land level is at some points ten to fifteen feet higher than the street, and to really appreciate how high that is, walk up the lane between Georgia and Union to see from the summit the drop down to Hawks Avenue. At the bottom of the lane at Hawks, the pavement is now lower than both Union and Georgia because as the hills were cut the hollows were filled.

Hawks Avenue developed later than other streets at this end of the neighbourhood. Both Campbell and Heatley avenues saw development in the early 1890s; by contrast, the first homes on Hawks Avenue were built in the 500-block in 1900. By 1908, the street was almost entirely built up, but instead of individual homes, most of the property owners built row housing. The brilliant green and red building on the east side of Hawks at the lane between Union and Georgia dates from 1905 and, in 1974, underwent an extensive renovation that cut balconies into the roof, among other modifications **(14)**. On the west side of Hawks at the lane is number 701-725, built in 1907 and in derelict condition by the 1970s; it was finally renovated in 1984-5. A few steps to the south are two buildings, also from 1905, referred to on early fire insurance maps as "cabins"; these buildings manage to squeeze nine units each onto a 25-foot by 122-

14. The row house at the northeast corner of Hawks and Union, before its renovation in the 1970s. (Photographer unknown, John Atkin collection)

foot lot. Other cabins in the neighbourhood were built with a long outside hallway running the length of the building, so that from the street it looks like an ordinary house (848 Union and 727 Keefer are good examples of this).

Walk north on Hawks to MacLean Park.

At the corner of Hawks and Georgia you can see, on the southeast corner, the addition to the house for a corner grocery store **(15)**; the corner entrance to the last unit of the rowhouses, 725 Hawks, identifies it as a former store, too. The neighbourhood had at one time many corner stores, selling groceries and baked goods, mostly located on the streetcar routes running along East Georgia and Campbell Avenue. Following the shutdown of the streetcar system and the shifting of the routes to Hastings, the stores gradually closed and today many have been converted into artists' studios.

Also at the corner is MacLean Park, named for Vancouver's first mayor; the original MacLean Park was at Union and Jackson until the

15. The building on the southeast corner of Hawks and Georgia, as it appeared in the 1970s when the addition still housed a grocery store.

(Photographer unknown, John Atkin collection)

1960s, when the city built public housing on it. In the 1950s and 1960s, North American cities were involved in a program of slum clearance and freeway building, known as urban renewal, and Vancouver was no different. An extensive network of freeways was planned for the city and the major downtown route was to slice through Strathcona. As the area between Main Street and Victoria Drive was considered a blighted area, it was to be cleared like a forest when the freeways went in, so that new "modern" housing could be built based on English and American models of public housing. Because the original MacLean Park was free of buildings, it was built on first, so that as other blocks of the neighbourhood were demolished, the residents could be moved into the new housing. To replace the park in the mid-1960s, an entire block of houses, an apartment building or two, and a bakery on the block bounded by Hawks, Heatley, Georgia and Keefer were demolished.

All that remains of the former block are the large trees that were part of the front garden of 796 Keefer, the home of William Harris. Other residents on the block in 1892 were Jesse James Dougan, the vice-principal of Strathcona School, Captain Frank Monk and Captain Wood. Captain Monk worked for the Union Steamship Company as master of the S.S. *Leonora*, a paddlesteamer of fifty-seven feet built in 1876 in Victoria, which did the Hastings Mill-to-Moodyville run. Later, the *Leonora* hauled stone intended for the paving of city streets. Captain Charles Moody, who lived at 870 Pender Street during the same time, was skipper of the Union Steamship Company's steam tug *Skidegate*, built in Victoria in 1879 as a cannery tender for use in the Queen Charlottes. Later Moody took command of the *Comox*, the first steel ship assembled in British Columbia (it was shipped in sections from the builders in Britain). Nearby, in the 800 block of Keefer Street, lived another Union Steamships man: Captain Absalom Freeman. Freeman served on such veterans of the company fleet as the *Skidegate*, *Capilano*, *Comox* and *Cutch*. This last vessel was the company's first "proper" ship, having been built as a pleasure craft in England in 1884 for the Maharajah of Cutch. The Maharajah's death soon after the ship's delivery saw it being used first for trade in the Gulf of Cutch and then by the German government in their East African operations before the

Union Steamship Company purchased it in 1890 and sailed it ten thousand miles to Vancouver. The *Cutch* served on the Vancouver-Nanaimo run for several years, before being transferred to the Alaska-Vancouver service, where it was wrecked in 1900.

Go east on Keefer for half a block, then return to Hawks and continue north.

At just about the mid-block point on the south side of the 800-block Keefer are two very tall houses that contrast with the lower and boxier homes around them. They were built just two years apart—856 in 1892 and 860 in 1894—from the same plans. Since then, 860 has suffered from a bad renovation with vinyl siding, new "heritage-style" aluminum windows and the loss of all its original decoration. By comparison, 856 Keefer is still in original condition **(16)**. The little pink house at 817 Keefer is picturesque in its decay.

The corner of Hawks and Keefer has a variety of buildings that demonstrate the random and unplanned nature of much of Strathcona. On the southeast corner is the much-added-to house that became Mr. Zanon's Montreal Bakery, with a retail outlet at the corner **(17)**; on the northwest corner is a small apartment building erected in 1906 **(18)**. Beside the latter are two well-maintained duplexes, built a few years earlier, that on first glance seem identical, both having black trim and asbestos shingles over the original siding. On closer inspection the subtle differences of rooflines and the size of the windows become apparent. The northern building is the older of the two, with narrower windows, coloured-glass insets surrounding the main pane in the bay windows, and a large gable in the roof instead of the dormer of its neighbour.

Across the street is 502-520 Hawks—six rental houses built in 1900 by Walter Scott, a store clerk at Gordon Drysdale's drygoods store, as an investment **(19)**. By 1986, a fire and a condemnation order from the city had reduced the original six houses to four, and the remaining ones were making a determined effort to fall down (one house, which had slipped off its meagre foundation of concrete blocks, was actually leaning on its neighbour). That year, however, they were purchased by a group of people brought together by an

16. (left) Early-1890s house at 856 Keefer Street.
17. (top right) The former location of the Montreal Bakery at the
southeast corner of Hawks and Keefer.
18. (bottom right) The northwest corner of Hawks and Keefer.

architect and a common interest in developing affordable housing for themselves. This group decided to rebuild the two lost houses at either end of the row, which meant designating the surviving four houses as heritage structures and placing restrictive covenants on the two new buildings.

The original four houses were gutted and raised to provide basements; new windows, roofs, and siding were added and lost porch brackets were replaced to complete the renovation/restoration. When the renovated houses were first painted, it was in a sombre colour scheme of medium grey with white trim for all of them (determined by scraping through ten coats of paint on the original siding and trim)—not the bright storybook colours currently used. When the project was completed, the property was strata-titled and the houses were sold back to the members of the group; for the first time since their construction they were individually owned. They are an interesting group: separate houses, yet with densities like an apartment building (a floor space ratio of over 1.5 for the site, and a net density of about forty units per acre).

These six houses have been erroneously described as CPR railway-workers' cottages. In fact, the first tenants, including Captain Alfred Bissett of the SS *Selkirk* in 512, butcher Harry Stuart in 516, and John Dawson, the circulation manager of the *Province* newspaper, in 508, show the diversity of occupations that could be found in this row and in the neighbourhood. (A similar row of houses, built in 1898 and now much modified, exists in the 400 block of Heatley.) A typical "worker's" house—a one-room cabin—still stands in the 300-block of Princess Street north of Hastings; once common near the Hastings Mill and other large industries, these buildings were sometimes grouped together on a single lot to provide cheap accommodation, but because of their small size few have survived.

If you walk up the lane south of the six houses, you will see several large houses facing Pender Street, but standing at the back of their lots. These houses were moved to the back so that rooming houses could be built at the front facing the street **(20)**. Farther along the lane there are two instances, at the rear of 828 and 834 East Pender, where the house remained in its original location and the rooming house was attached to its facade.

19. A collage of the six houses on Hawks Avenue as they originally stood before fires,

Quite possibly the rarest and most important houses in Strathcona, each a real gem, are the three across the street from the colourful six in the 500-block Hawks. Numbers 507, 515 and 521 Hawks were built in 1903 by the yard foreman of the Hastings Mill, Stanislaus Brereton, and are the earliest-known examples of the B.C. Mills, Timber and Trading Company prefabricated building system **(21)**. Invented and patented in 1904 by Edwin C. Mahony, manager of the Royal City Mills branch of the company, the system was introduced to the public at the 1904 Dominion Exhibition in Winnipeg. The houses were constructed of two- and four-foot-wide panels of clapboard, studs, and insulation that were bolted together with other panels to form walls. The houses came complete with doors and windows incorporated into the panels, flooring and roofing; even an iron chimney was available. They were designed to be permanent structures, unlike other prefabricated buildings that were intended to be knocked down after more substantial accommodation had been built, and were known for their quality and for being "free from annoying drafts." The company offered a variety of buildings ranging from a simple one-room house ("Model A," 11 feet square) to churches and schools. The Bank of Commerce used the BCMT&T system for many of its branches, one of which survives in Mission as the museum. Some of the BCMT&T

demolitions and restoration. (Photographer unknown, John Atkin collection)

20. Houses along the lane south of the 800-block East Pender.

buildings were shipped to San Francisco after the 1906 earthquake.

These three houses have been described as the experimental prototypes for the "prefab" system, which stayed in production until 1910. Brereton himself lived in 521 for a number of years. Although 507 has been refaced with stucco and defaced with aluminum windows and the others have had minor alterations, enough of their historic character survives to make them significant heritage houses.

Strathcona's unique diversity and heritage have been recognized by its residents since the late 1960s, when the Strathcona Property Owners and Tenants Association (SPOTA) formed to resist urban renewal and the planned Vancouver freeway system, only one piece of which—the Georgia Viaduct—had actually been built. The fight to save not only Strathcona but Gastown and Chinatown from freeways and urban renewal was central to the defeat of the conservative city government in 1972.

As we have seen, Strathcona developed in a random pattern, with individual property owners building what they wanted or needed. The houses, apartment buildings, and commercial uses managed to coexist side by side until after the Second World War, when

21. The BCMT&T prefabs on the west side of Hawks Avenue, showing the characteristic panels separated by battens.

the eye of the professional planner looked at the community and was horrified. Strathcona manages to break almost all the rules that apply to density, livability, the mixing of uses, light, space, and setbacks, but because the rules were broken by people unaware that there *were* rules, Strathcona has remained a very livable place. Those rules must continue to be broken if new construction is to take place in a compatible fashion; renovation and restoration of existing houses must not become such a nightmare for owners that demolition is the only option. Experience elsewhere in the city has shown that the elaborate sets of rules and codes making up zoning and building by-laws ensure that Vancouver Specials are the only houses that get built. Strathcona is fragile; one or two inappropriate houses per block is all that it takes to upset the balance and forever alter the historic character. Conversely, it would be disastrous to have Strathcona restored to a picture-perfect Victorian "Disneyland set," an alteration to the historic character almost as severe as the Vancouver Special.

Coffee Shops of the Downtown Eastside

1 ½ HOURS

I n the years around the First World War, the Downtown Eastside was the cultural and civic centre for Vancouver. It supported live theatres with enough seats for over eight thousand patrons and some of the largest stages west of Chicago, numerous movie houses, and the main branch of the public library, as well as City Hall.

In the decades since, because of the westward move of today's downtown and the resulting lack of economic activity, the Downtown Eastside has evolved into a neighbourhood that offers an affordable home to many. The hotels, once a stop for travellers, now provide shelter for many of the area's residents and, in many cases, recent construction has been devoted to erecting or converting existing buildings into housing.

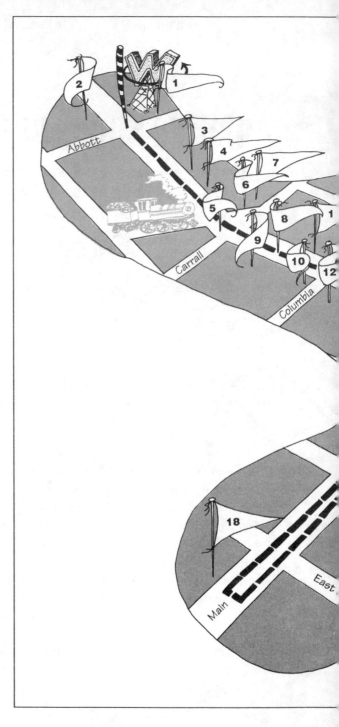

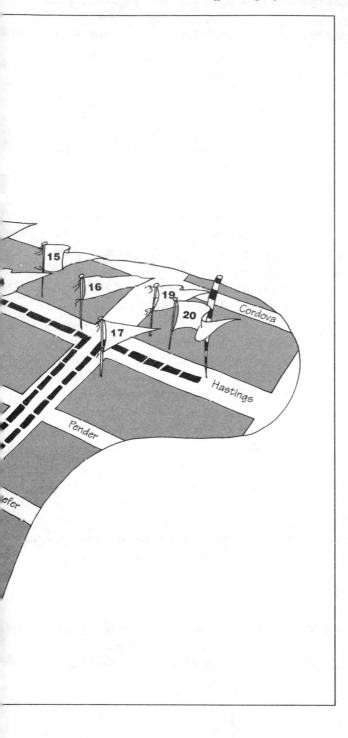

However, after twenty-five years of frantic growth, today's downtown is moving east again and, with the completion of the new B.C. Hydro Building at Dunsmuir and Homer, the continuing development of the Concord Pacific properties on the old Expo Lands, and development around the CN Station on Main Street, the stability of the Downtown Eastside neighbourhood is looking dubious. Without careful direction, these new pressures may disrupt and displace both the architecture and the residents.

Frequently called "skid road," the Downtown Eastside makes many Vancouverites uncomfortable, yet it has hidden delights that are often overlooked in the rush along Hastings Street between the modern downtown and the eastern suburbs. In 1886, when the Town of Granville became the City of Vancouver, the centre of the city was the intersection of Water and Carrall streets; Maple Tree Square still had its tree, commemorated in 1925 with a plaque placed by the Vancouver Pioneers Association. After the destruction of the city in the great fire of June, 1886, and the arrival of the Canadian Pacific Railway a year later, the city—prompted by the activities of some major land speculators—expanded rapidly. The Oppenheimers, originally merchants in Victoria, had owned land in the area since the 1870s. By 1884, they were clearing and subdividing their holdings from Carrall Street east as far as Gore Avenue into twenty-five-foot lots. (Gore Avenue is the original skid road for logs being moved to the shore of the Inlet at the Hastings Mill; as this took place before the CPR's 1885 street survey, Gore does not conform to the street grid.)

In the years after the railway's arrival, there was a tug-of-war between eastside business interests (primarily the Oppenheimers) and the Canadian Pacific Railway, which in 1884 received from the provincial government a land grant of almost half of the downtown peninsula, as well as land to the south of False Creek—in all, over six thousand acres. To entice business to its part of the forest, the CPR in 1886 constructed the first Hotel Vancouver at Georgia and Granville.

A year later, Frank W. Hart bought a roller rink in Port Moody (which was being abandoned by most of its residents, who were following the railway west to Vancouver), dismantled it and shipped it to eastside Vancouver to provide the city with its first legitimate theatre. This canvas-roofed building was reassembled on Carrall Street south of Pender on what was then the edge of False Creek; it could accommodate eight hundred people sitting on benches or 250 roller-skaters. Hart's theatre hosted Salvation Army meetings, boxing matches (including an 1888 one at which the Marquis of Queensbury refereed) and theatricals. Frank Hart himself is remembered for sporting Vancouver's first silk top hat and was one of the city's first undertakers; after leaving Vancouver, he speculated in town futures in Alaska for a while before becoming a successful furniture merchant in Prince Rupert. In 1891, the CPR went into competition with Hart by erecting the Vancouver Opera House, a lavish theatre of over twelve hundred seats which soon was featuring such theatrical luminaries as Thomas Keene, Sir Henry Irving and Sarah Bernhardt—"the finest talent European and American stages had to offer." (Later known as the Orpheum and finally as the Lyric, the opera house survived until the late 1960s, when it was pulled down to make way for a new Eaton's department store.)

The Oppenheimers, through their Vancouver Improvement Company, and C.D. Rand, a major real-estate investor, were instrumental in establishing the Vancouver streetcar system in 1890. The Powell Street line ran from Granville and Pender to Hastings, Cambie, Cordova and along Powell to Campbell Avenue; the Westminster (Main Street) line started at 2nd Avenue, crossing False Creek on a trolley bridge built on the west side of the road bridge to Powell, from where it used the Powell line to Granville and then continued to Pacific Street. Not surprisingly, its route was chosen to run through the Oppenheimers' extensive land holdings in the eastern part of the city. A year later, other investors incorporated the Westminster and Vancouver Tramway Company to run from Vancouver to New Westminster.

In the depression of 1893, these transit companies got into major financial trouble; the streetcar system was even offered to the City of Vancouver, which rejected it following a referendum. Four years later, though, after an infusion of English capital, another syndicate formed the B.C. Electric Railway Company and took over operations of the street railway. The BCER built its head office in 1898 at the southwest corner of Hastings and Carrall; in 1912, the architects Somervell and Putnam designed, for the same site, a grander building combining the head office with an interurban railway terminus.

This building was to have a major impact on the surrounding area. Despite the westward shift of the business district, which began in earnest around 1910 with the erection of the new courthouse on Georgia, the BCER's head office and interurban station put thousands of people per day onto the Downtown Eastside streets, ensuring a continuing and lively street life. For decades, numerous small businesses thrived in the area. However, in 1957, the BCER opened its new office building at Burrard and Nelson, completing a transition that had seen interurban systems dismantled and city services converted "from rails to rubber." For the Downtown Eastside, this meant a loss of vital pedestrian traffic; coupled with the termination of North Shore ferry service in 1958, it delivered a blow from which the area has never fully recovered.

This economic downturn resulted in very little development pressure on the Downtown Eastside, leaving much of the architecture intact. Along with several blocks of the Victory Square area to the west and parts of Chinatown to the south, the Downtown Eastside survives today as an enclave of individuality—of small buildings erected by individual owners on twenty-five-foot lots, providing for varied and interesting streetscapes of shop fronts. The modern Downtown has lost this type of streetscape over the years; even Gastown, although home to many distinctive buildings, is in essence an Edwardian-era warehouse district, dominated by the large masonry edifices of wholesale grocery operations such as Malkin's and Kelly-Douglas. The appreciation of detail is much finer in the Downtown Eastside—for example, the Empress Hotel at 225 East Hastings, although occupying only a single twenty-five-foot lot, has an almost monumental presence on the street.

While many of the smaller businesses did not survive the demise of the BCER station, the coffee shops of Hastings Street have continued in operation by serving local customers. Almost all of those remaining are from the 1940s, the heyday of coffee-shop design, and against all odds their neon, counters, stools, booths and tessellation remain intact, offering a unique view of the recent past.

Not so fortunate were the numerous theatres, vaudeville palaces, and movie houses. One or two have survived intact; a few remain as stripped-down shells that have been put to other uses, but most were demolished.

Start at Abbott Street, in front of one of the great building projects of Hastings Street: the Woodward's department store.

Charles Woodward migrated west from Ontario in 1892 and established his first Vancouver store at the northeast corner of Main and East Georgia. After ten years, his business had grown to the point that he began to search for larger premises, and he chose the northwest corner of Abbott and Hastings street for the new four-storey brick "department store"—a relatively new idea for the time. (Canadian precedents for this type of operation were Timothy Eaton's emporium on Yonge Street in Toronto and David Spencer's elegant complex in Victoria, both dating from the 1860s; much more usual were individually owned specialty stores, selling meat but not produce, or pharmaceuticals but not stationery.) The site, which was then a swamp almost eight feet below street level, was chosen because Vancouver's principal shopping street, Cordova, was considered to be too expensive.

By 1908 the store had expanded into six storeys designed by architect George Wenyon. This portion still exists as part of the much larger store you see today, as the Woodward's master plan from the 1930s was never realized. Instead, over the years, the store has had more than a dozen additions to it, so that it now takes up about half the block.

Along with the expansions to the store came a need to provide automobile parking, which was accommodated in a garage on Cordova Street—no longer the significant shopping street in the city since the advent of the automobile era. One part of this parkade, erected in 1946, resulted in the demolition of an early theatre and restaurant building dating from 1898. The Grand Theatre, which occupied the second floor of the building, featured vaudeville and magic lantern tricks, while the Savoy Restaurant below was an early and fashionable venture of Cavaliere Agostino Gabriele Ferrera. The Woodward's parking garage itself expanded to the point that, by 1957, it had the dubious honour of being the largest in the Commonwealth.

Although much of the rest of Vancouver, with its demolition of old landmarks and their replacement by new architecture, is making the effort to look like everywhere else, one object—the Woodward's "W"—sticks up on the skyline to remind everyone that this is indeed Vancouver. The sixteen-foot-tall, six-thousand-pound red-neon letter, almost three hundred feet above the street, has been revolving six times a minute above the store for thirty years. It sits on an eighty-foot-tall replica of the Eiffel Tower, erected as an advertising gimmick in 1927, which itself perches on a five-storey structure built to house two twenty-five-thousand-gallon gravity-feed water tanks, elevator machinery, and until 1980 the store's peanut-butter factory.

Originally, a light was mounted on top of the tower—not just any ordinary light, but a forty-eight-inch-diameter searchlight of two million candlepower, which, on clear nights, could be seen on Vancouver Island. In 1941, during the Second World War, the federal government doused the light, fearing that pilots would confuse Woodward's with the airport at Sea Island. The revolving "W" was added in the 1950s and is one of the last of a number of objects, including water

1. (left) *The Woodward's "W" atop the store on Hastings Street.*
2. (right) *The White Lunch at 126 West Hastings, as it appeared about 1970.*
(Photographer unknown, City of Vancouver Planning Department)

tanks, loaves of bread and giant shoes, that could be seen on the rooftops of the city **(1)**.

Two years after Charles Woodward moved to Hastings Street, Mr. Bancroft opened the Bismarck Cafe on the southwest corner of Abbott and Hastings. The Bismarck featured a full orchestra, seating for 115 people, eight private dining rooms for ladies and one electric fountain. It became a billiard hall and bowling alley in the 1940s and today it is a shoe store. A longer-surviving landmark on Hastings was the White Lunch, a tenant until the 1970s in the Ralph Block at 126 West Hastings **(2)**.

Walk east along Hastings Street on the north side.

The former Wosk's furniture store at 68 West Hastings is all that remains of the Columbia Theatre, a vaudeville house. Across the street from it, on the north side, the Army and Navy store occupies two buildings **(3)**; the lower eastern one, clad in blue metal panels, is the remains of the Rex Theatre, a lavish venue that is reputed to have been Vancouver's fastest construction job, as it opened for business twenty minutes after the last coat of paint had been applied **(4)**. The theatre was bought by the Cohen family and was operated as a movie house for a few years until the building was gutted and converted into Army and Navy store space. The Cordova Street side of the store occupies the 1889 Lonsdale Block, built by Thomas Dunn and Jonathan Miller; the former had his hardware store in the building. The latter, who had been a resident of Burrard Inlet since the 1860s and had served as constable before the city's incorporation, was a wealthy landowner and developer.

Back on the south side of Hastings, next to Fields, is a large gap in the streetwall. The vacant space was, until the 1970s, the Pantages Theatre, built in 1917 by Alexander Pantages to replace his earlier theatre farther east on the street. At the height of his career, Pantages owned some thirty theatres across North America and operated another forty-six. A waiter in Dawson City during the Klondike gold rush of the late 1890s, Pantages broke into the entertainment business by organizing pastimes in the saloons. After returning from the Yukon to Seattle in 1902, he built his first theatre, the Crystal; the

3. *Looking east on Hastings Street around the turn of the century. The F. Buscombe and Company building is now the western part of the Army and Navy Department Store at 27 West Hastings. The Romanesque building adjoining it on the eastern side was demolished and replaced by the Rex Theatre. The Palace Hotel building still exists, although its main floor has been filled in for shops.* (Photographer unknown, VPL 5249)

next was Vancouver's first Pantages, erected at 142 East Hastings in 1906. Eleven years later, he completed his second Vancouver theatre—an elegant, ornate white terracotta "palace" that cost $350,000 and could seat two thousand patrons at a time **(5)**.

The eventual collapse of the Pantages empire was due in part to his failure, as an independent, to secure motion pictures for his theatres (another reason was undoubtedly the sensational civil charge laid against him in 1929 that he had raped a would-be chorus girl; Pantages eventually settled out of court for $3,000). Movie studios of the day built and operated their own theatres to screen their epics, so

4. *The north side of Hastings Street west of Carrall, showing, on the left, a portion of the Rex Theatre—now the eastern side of the Army and Navy Department Store—and, on the right, the edge of the Merchants' Bank Building.*
(Photographer unknown, VPL 20988)

independents, such as the Pantages and the Stanley on Granville, varied their fare by alternating movie screenings with vaudeville performances and local theatre productions. One highlight of the Pantages's career as a vaudeville house was the appearance there in 1934 of Texas Guinan, the Queen of the New York Speakeasies (who had recently been put out of business in the United States by the repeal of Prohibition). In the "Roaring Twenties," seated on a piano and wearing a huge chrysanthemum or cabbage rose pinned to an available piece of her low-cut dress, she presided over her New York establishment and perfected a breezy repartee with her high-rolling customers. She coined the sarcastic phrase, which has since fallen from common parlance, that a big spender was "a big butter and egg man" after determining that one self-important customer had made his fortune in dairying and poultry. Vancouver saw the last appearance of Guinan and her troupe of dancing girls; she became sick here and died in Vancouver General Hospital.

Pantages sold his theatre chain to Warner Brothers and R.K.O. Studios in the late 1930s. In 1946, by which time the building was known as the Beacon, ownership passed to Odeon Theatres, which

5. *Looking west on Hastings Street from Carrall in the mid-1920s, with the newly completed Cenotaph at Victory Square visible in the distance. The Pantages Theatre is on the left, and the Merchants' Bank Building on the right has been taken over by the Bank of Montreal. Also visible is the Canadian Pacific Railway company's crossing gates and track (where the pedestrian is walking) and the switcher's shack on the extreme left.*

spent over $100,000 renovating it, "combining classical architecture of the old with the latest in interior fittings." The new Hastings Odeon neon sign was over forty feet tall. The building ended its days as the Majestic, and, although the owners had no immediate use for the site, the building was demolished to avoid taxes. The cherubs that once graced the parapet can be found today in the garden of the Vancouver Museum in Vanier Park on Kitsilano Point.

The second Pantages Theatre was built on the site of the Panama Theatre and the Winter Cafe; if you look closely at the west wall of the Burns Block at 18 West Hastings, now home to Budget Printing, you can see the last vestige of the Panama Theatre, a heavy granite and sandstone column, still clinging to its wall.

At the southwest corner of Hastings and Carrall stands the above-mentioned B.C. Electric Railway head-office building and interurban station, in use since the late 1950s as a branch of the Bank of Montreal. The ground floor was open on the Hastings Street side to allow access for the electric trains which travelled over the Central Park line to New Westminster and Chilliwack. The interurban system was the most extensive in Canada—of the same scale and efficiency as the legendary "Big Red Cars" of old Los Angeles, and just as doomed. The Vancouver-Chilliwack line was just one portion of the system; another line connected Commercial Drive near 1st Avenue with New Westminster via Burnaby Lake; a third ran from the north end of Granville Bridge, through Kitsilano and Kerrisdale to Marpole, crossed the Fraser River and traversed rural Richmond on its way to Steveston; yet another line followed the North Arm of the Fraser River between New Westminster and Marpole.

Across the street from the former interurban station is Pioneer Square, usually known as Pigeon Park, which was part of an old CPR right-of-way connecting the False Creek railyards with the main line on Burrard Inlet. Looking northeast and southwest from the park, you can see the "cut" through to Gastown and back towards False Creek, where the buildings were fitted around the old right-of-way. The CPR ran and shunted its trains along the track, creating monumental traffic tie-ups on Hastings Street until the 1930s, when it dug the Dunsmuir Tunnel, now the route of the SkyTrain system.

Although imposing as it stands, the Merchants' Bank Building which fronts onto the park is merely the base of a projected seven-storey building; it was built in 1913 to the designs of Somervell and Putnam, who the previous year had completed the BCER Building across the street. The latter was to have had a steep copper roof, and if the two buildings had been completed as designed, they would have made a handsome pair, anchoring what had been the southeast corner of the 1870 Granville Townsite (the bend in Hastings Street at Carrall is due to the 1870 survey abutting the CPR's 1885 survey).

The Merchants' Bank Building eventually became a branch of the Bank of Montreal. In 1940, to expand the premises, the Bank of Montreal demolished the building adjoining it on its north side; it had originally been the Bijou Family Theatre, and advertised: "We cater to Ladies and Children—Admission 5 cents." Lamenting the loss of the old building, the *Province* remarked, "One of Vancouver's oldest landmarks will be razed—the unpretentious little building at 333 Carrall which once housed the Bijou Theatre will be demolished to make way for a modern one-storey building....The building was one of the first to be built after the fire of 1886." During the demolition, the building next door, originally the Louvre Saloon and Hotel, lost the portion that turned the corner to meet the Bijou's facade **(6)**.

Reinhold Minarty was the proprietor of the Louvre in the 1890s; some years later, the Gaerdes Brothers took over the operation, with Herman managing what had by then become the Louvre Cafe while John looked after the hotel upstairs. On the wall at the lane you can still make out the faded signage for the saloon and hotel, advertising beds at twenty cents a night **(7)**. The bank's "modern" building, which today is home to a sandwich shop, still stands.

Cross Hastings and Carrall streets and continue east along the south side of Hastings.

Crossing both Carrall and Hastings streets puts you on the southeast corner of the block, in front of the 1906 Pennsylvania Hotel, which in the past thirty-five years has lost its corner turret and most of its charm. A few steps to its east is the Holden Building at 16 East Hastings, the third of the trio of impressive office buildings (along with the B.C. Electric and Merchants' Bank buildings) which, in the palmy

6. *The Bijou and the Louvre at Hastings and Carrall, with a portion of the CPR's crossing sign visible on the right.* (Photographer unknown, VPL 1262)

*7. The Louvre Hotel wall facing into the alley north of Hastings Street,
showing room rates and advertising.*

days before the First World War, almost set a standard for the Hastings
and Carrall area. A chunky Edwardian Commercial tower, it was
designed by W.T. Whiteway as an office building and bank and constructed in 1910. The Holden Building served in the years from 1929
to 1936 as Vancouver's City Hall; as the city administration expanded
with municipal growth in the 1920s and the annexation of the munic-
ipalities of South Vancouver and Point Grey in 1929, it overflowed
the old City Hall, which had for thirty years been occupying the converted theatre at the rear of the 1888 market building on Main Street
just south of the Carnegie Library. After 1936, when the current City
Hall opened at 12th and Cambie, all trace of city occupation,
including a temporary council chamber, was removed from the
Holden Building, allowing it to revert to its former status as a modest
office building. However, as the decades passed, the changing nature
of the area made a new use for it opportune. In the 1980s, the
Downtown Eastside Residents Association restored the exterior, renovated the interior into housing, and renamed it the Tellier Tower **(8)**.

Such large buildings as the Tellier Tower are the exception in the
area, as a lot is more likely to be occupied by a cafe in a small building;
the proximity of the interurban station (which itself had a Honey Dew
stand still remembered fondly by some Vancouverites) supported a
myriad of them. One of the most renowned, the Only Seafood Cafe at
20 East Hastings, is a few steps to the east of the Tellier Tower. The
Mexican Jewellery Palace was the original tenant in this location, and
the first restaurant in the building, The Vancouver Oyster Saloon,

8. *Looking west on Hastings towards Carrall about 1915. The large building on the left with the cigar advertisement painted on its side is the Holden Building, now known as the Tellier Tower. The white building at the corner with the large portal is the B.C. Electric Railway Company head office and interurban depot. Also visible is the Panama Theatre (the third building past the corner), demolished in 1917 to make way for the Pantages Theatre.* (Photographer unknown, John Atkin collection)

9. *The neon sign of the Only at 20 East Hastings.*

opened in 1916. It was later bought by Nic Thodas who named it after himself; in 1923, when his brother joined him, it became the Nic and Gus. Finally, in 1924, it became the Only, which in the decades since has become something of a Vancouver institution. The Only still has no public washroom, the fish is still packed on ice in the window, and seating is limited to about twenty. The tin ceiling, now heavily painted over, is original, but the mural was painted in 1985 for the following year's Expo; outside, the neon sign is a good example of 1930s design **(9)**.

Yet another cafe, now vanished, was Low's Waffle House—where "all waffles are homemade" and "exclusive" and cost ten cents—at 28 East Hastings. To the east at number 30 was the English Kitchen (Nic D. Panagopolous, Proprietor) which, prior to their purchase of the Only, employed the Thodas brothers. (Restaurant employment was one of the few opportunities open to the Greeks who immigrated to Vancouver in the 1920s; the above-mentioned Mr. Bancroft of the Bismarck Cafe was described in *Vancouver Illustrated* as a native of Greece, fluent in four languages, and the president of the Vancouver

10. *The Empire Rooms, at the southwest corner of Hastings and Columbia, in the 1920s. The building was demolished after the Second World War, and a modern bank building now occupies the site.* (Photographer unknown, VPL 11469)

11. *The north side of Hastings Street just to the west of Columbia Street in the 1940s, showing the White Lunch and the Princess Theatre before its art deco transformation.* (Photographer unknown, VPL 5085)

Greek Association.) Until it was demolished some years ago, 30 East Hastings had an upper floor, rented out to roomers. If you walked east along this block in 1935, you could have eaten in the Common Gold Cafe at number 50, had coffee at either the Log Cabin Lunch at number 54 or the Savoy at number 66, or enjoyed pie and ice cream in the Empire at the corner of Columbia and East Hastings **(10)**.

The building at 65 East Hastings was the location of one of the numerous and popular White Lunch cafes **(11)**, the first of which opened opposite Woodward's around the beginning of the First World War. Over the years, the cafeteria-style White Lunches in Vancouver and Victoria became popular with the likes of Premier John Oliver, who enjoyed pushing his tray along the counter because, as he once said, "I like to see and pick what I'm going to eat." This location, notable for its black and white and chrome interior, was open twenty-four hours a day with seats for 150 people. Like the Aristocratic coffee-shop chain in Vancouver, which had distinctive 1930s-era "Puttin' on the Ritz" typography and neon and the stylized character "Risty" as a mascot, the White Lunch chain developed elaborate and sophisticated signs. From the first White Lunches using rela-

12. McDonough Hall, at the southeast corner of Hastings and Columbia.

tively simple signs with light bulbs to outline letters, they advanced to state-of-the-art neon, creating the memorable revolving coffee cup and elegant silhouetted waiters and other characters of later years.

A surviving landmark on the north side of the street, with something of the same design pedigree as the stylish coffee shops of the 1930s and 1940s, is the Lux Theatre. Its art deco facade dates from the 1940s and covered a much plainer one on the old Princess Theatre.

On the southeast corner of Columbia and East Hastings is the Cozy Corner Grocery, one of the few surviving wood-frame buildings on the street. City archivist Major Matthews claimed that it was built in 1888 on land valued at $355 for the St. Andrews and Caledonian Society, it was named McDonough Hall and was the site soon thereafter of a grand masked ball, reputed to have been the first in Vancouver. The building's angled corner bay is an unusual design feature—square bay windows were typical of the Stick and Eastlake architecture of the 1860s and 1870s, and most of the examples of the style built in the Lower Mainland were demolished years ago **(12)**. Earlier tenants in the building included a tailor's shop, the Horse Shoe

13. *The Broadway Cafe in the 1920s; the storefront is now occupied by a grocery store.* (Photographer unknown, VPL 7462)

Barber Shop, and the Deluxe Fruit and Vegetable Company. During the Depression of the 1930s, the Water Street Mission occupied the hall upstairs and ministered to the unemployed and impoverished who flocked into Vancouver.

The sleazy Sunrise Hotel on the northeast corner of Columbia and Hastings demonstrates as well as any building on the street the declining fortunes of the area; in better days, it was the Hotel Irving, touted as "the newest and finest" hotel in town when it was erected in 1906, with a cafe that seated eighty people. The pilasters on the hotel's facade have since lost their Ionic capitals; also gone are the decorative cornice and pediment. The cafe had competition from the Broadway Cafe next door, an elegant little place advertised as "Vancouver's Deluxe Cafe," similar to the Bismarck Cafe a few blocks to the west **(13)**. The Broadway's building is now a grocery store.

The existence of all these cafes within a couple of blocks demonstrates how many travellers there were, especially salesmen staying in the many hotels lining Hastings Street and probably plying their trade in the Gastown warehouse district or among the businesses along the industrial waterfront. In the decades before the 1950s, businesses such as Malkin's and Kelly-Douglas in Gastown were the centre of the wholesale produce and grocery business in the city—at least, the white-controlled portion of it (the alleged extent of Chinese control of the produce business during the 1930s prompted a virulent campaign by some politicians and labour leaders against the Chinese Fruit and Vegetable Merchants Association). The large number of brothels in the area during the 1920s and 1930s also contributed to the amount of street traffic.

On the south side of the street, the Radio Lunch (presumably named because you could listen to the radio serials while eating your cereal) stood at 108 East Hastings, the New Glasgow Cafe stood at number 123 1/2, and the only survivor of them all—the Blue Eagle Cafe—has occupied 130 East Hastings since 1944. For several years before 1944, the New Atlantic Cafe occupied that storefront, having taken it over from one of the original White Lunches. The interior of the Blue Eagle is quite a treat. On the walls are ornate green-tinged tiles and the floor is laid with hexagonal tiles in a floral pattern. At the entrance, the name Blue Eagle is incorporated into the floor tiling; outside is a type of neon sign, with tubes fastened to a metal frame suspended above the door, that has all but disappeared in Vancouver **(14)**.

Next door, the tessellation at the entrance to Universal News reads B.C. Tailoring, dating from the building's use before it became a billiard hall in the thirties. One door farther to the east you can see the partially hidden tile pattern surviving from the Golden Gate Cafe, where Gus Thodas of the Only was once proprietor. Across the street is one of the nicest survivors of "that garish jungle of neon and cheap tile that marks the loggers' end of Hastings Street," as Pierre Berton described the Downtown Eastside in a 1950s article in *Mayfair*, "Canada's Smartest Magazine." The Balmoral Hotel sign is over five storeys tall with flashing light bulbs, deep red neon tubes and a clock at the bottom. A more modest piece of neon adorns the Hotel Washington just up the street: it is a small, simple sign of a type that could be found throughout downtown Vancouver—a standard design that just needed tubes in the business name to complete the sign **(15)**.

Vancouver was noted across North America for its wealth of neon. By the 1950s, the city had more linear feet of neon than anywhere else in the world except possibly Shanghai. Granville Street was identified on postcards as the "Great White Way" and Hastings Street was not far behind. The clutter and sheer number and type of signs echoed the turn-of-the-century practice of attaching advertising to everything; it was only in the mid-sixties that city authorities began to frown on such clutter on the street. The 1970s was a period of anti-billboard by-laws and beautification efforts in many major cities, and neon did not fare well at all. As business districts declined and their nature changed, neon became the scapegoat for a variety of social ills—everything from prostitution to the litter problem. In Vancouver, many of the best signs were lost in the effort to clean up the streets. However, the new problem of lifeless downtown districts can be partially attributed to the lack of ambient light, which used to be provided by neon signs, especially on rain-soaked nights when the

14. (left) *The Blue Eagle cafe at 130 East Hastings.*
15. (right) *The neon signs for the hotels Washington and Balmoral.*

16. Looking west on Hastings Street, from a point near Main, in
November, 1934, when the Pantages Theatre was known as the Royal.
(Photographer unknown, VPL 19635)

reflections provided a colourful display on the pavement. Although
there has been a revival of neon manufacturing and display, the days
of the big spectaculars are gone and the survivors are continually
falling victim to development.

Across the street from the Balmoral and the Washington, at 142
East Hastings, is the Pantages Theatre. As mentioned above, it was
Alexander Pantages's first theatre in Vancouver, built in 1906 with
750 seats. It is reputed to be the oldest intact, continuously operating
theatre in the province. After his new theatre was completed,
Pantages sold this one to Charles Royal in 1917 **(16)**. As the Royal, it
made news in 1933 because of a bombing; the building had been
rented to the Workers Unity League for a meeting, during which a
bomb went off, destroying not only the entire front lobby but
breaking windows on the ninth floor of the Balmoral Hotel.
Following its repair, the Royal became the State Theatre and operated as a burlesque house; its name then changed for a time to the
Queen's; after more renovations in 1945, it became a movie house
once again named the State Theatre. Within the first year of operation the management was fined $1,000 for charging more than the

Wartime Prices Board permitted. An appeal reduced the fine to $50.

In 1952 the theatre became the Avon, home to the Everyman Repertory Company. Their first production was *Macbeth*. The next production—Erskine Caldwell's *Tobacco Road*—brought the theatre back into the limelight. The vice squad viewed a performance and deemed the play "indecent, immoral and obscene"; the cast and crew were arrested and the trial made international headlines. Even though the playwright appeared for the defense, the theatre company was found guilty, but it received only a $20 fine. In the 1970s, the theatre, renamed City Nights, reverted to showing movies; after a brief closure it continues today as the Sung Sing, showing Chinese films.

At the corner of Hastings and Main streets is the Carnegie Centre, one of Vancouver's most-used community centres. As you approach the corner, you pass the ornate and colourful stained-glass windows illuminating its inside stairwell. The windows, designed by Toronto artist N.T. Lyon, show full portraits of Shakespeare, Milton and Spenser in the top portion and in the bottom, three head-and-shoulder portraits of Burns, Scott and Moore. These three bottom windows were returned to the building in the mid-1980s after being discovered in a basement.

Carnegie Centre was designed by George W. Grant and built in 1903 as the City's main library. It was funded by American industrialist Andrew Carnegie who, after amassing his fortune in steel, started giving it away to provide libraries bearing his name to English-speaking communities around the world. The building also served as the city museum and archives and remained so for about ten years after the library moved to Burrard Street in 1957; it then sat empty for a few years before being renovated and expanded in the 1970s into the much-needed community resource it is today. A 1991 grant from the B.C. Heritage Trust has restored the roof to its original appearance using standing-seam copper panels.

Also worthy of note, not because of any real architectural or historical significance, but because it is there, is one of the city's two underground public conveniences, in front of the Carnegie Centre (the other is at Hamilton and Hastings). While it may seem rash to venture down the stairs, those who do are pleasantly surprised to find some of the cleanest bathrooms in Vancouver.

Cross the Main and Hastings intersection to reach the southeast corner.

This corner and its buildings reflect the prominence that this part of town once had; the imposing Dawson Building is to the northwest, the Library to the southwest, the Royal Bank's East End Branch on the southeast corner and the Bank of Montreal's essay in neoclassicism on the northeast corner. This was the civic and business centre of Vancouver for many years, and the provincial court and jail, along with the police station, still remain on the few blocks north of the intersection.

The interesting addition to the Royal Bank, which is one large arch that is both window and entrance and mimics the main building's many window arches between its Ionic columns, was built on the site of the Four Ten Coffee Shop **(17)**.

Walk south on Main Street.

Like Hastings, Main Street was home to a number of Vancouver's early theatres. A few blocks south of Hastings, in the 700 block between Union and East Georgia, stood the Avenue and Imperial theatres. The Avenue, at 711 Main, was the site in 1915 of the local premiere of D.W. Griffiths' blockbuster film *Birth of a Nation*. The theatre was home for a time to the Vancouver Light Opera Company, and the renowned Irish tenor John McCormack sang on its stage **(18)**. In 1933, when a fire broke out next door at the Standard Junk Company, the orchestra continued playing to allay any possible panic as nearly a thousand

17. *The Four-Ten coffee shop at 410 Main Street in the 1970s.*
(Photographer unknown, John Atkin collection)

patrons left the theatre. It was demolished in 1936 for the construction of the Electrical Substation you see now, in itself a fine building.

The Imperial, across the street at 720 Main, was built in 1912 at a cost of $60,000 by the Canadian Theatre and Amusement Company. It later became a Chinese theatre, importing Chinese Opera and producing classical Chinese plays. That use was short-lived, however, and in 1927 it became the Pyramid Temple and in 1930 the Pentecostal Emmanuel Temple. By 1934, when it passed into the possession of the city, probably for nonpayment of taxes, workers were surprised to find the building had been stripped bare of everything moveable, including flooring. In 1939, Welsh's Auto Wrecking moved in and stayed until 1966 when the building became a theatre again, this time showing pornographic films. Apart from the ugly stucco and loss of the entrance canopy, the exterior has remained intact.

Go north on Main Street to Hastings Street and walk east on the north side.

18. *The interior of the Avenue Theatre in the 1920s.*
(Photographer unknown, VPL 6628)

19. The Empress Hotel at 235 East Hastings.

The eight-storey Empress Hotel at 235 East Hastings, built in 1912, has a monumental appearance, in part because of the narrow twenty-five-foot lot on which it is built **(19)**. The beer parlour on the ground floor has an interesting tile floor and neon signs inside marking the Ladies and Gents entrances, in turquoise and pink, the same colours as the large projecting sign. In this block the Economy Cafe, the New Star Cafe and Crescent Cafe could be found. Number 239 East Hastings is a pleasant-looking wood-framed building from 1903, designed by Blackmore and Son; Blackmore senior was responsible for the 1891 Strathcona School.

On the sidewall of the Afton Hotel you can see the faded remains of a sign advising that "Jo-To Stops Stomach Suffering" **(20)**; Jo-To was one of the many products of Dr. Middleton's Food Products Company, whose offices were at 850 East Hastings. Besides Jo-To, the company produced Genuine Ironized Whole Wheat Flour, Blue Ribbon White Bread and "delicious macaroons and cookies." President Thomas Polson lived at 5375 Angus Drive in Third Shaughnessy (see Chapter Seven).

The Afton Hotel was designed in 1912 by Arthur Julius Bird, who for a time was the city's architect and designed the Coroner's Court Building (now home to the Police Museum) on Cordova

*20. The Afton Hotel, with the Jo-To sign still visible on its sidewall,
and the Ovaltine Cafe at 251 East Hastings.*

Street and Fire Hall Number 6 in the West End—the first in North America to be designed specifically for motorized equipment. In private practice he designed numerous spacious apartment buildings, including Salsbury Court at 1010 Salsbury Drive. On the Afton, the oversized sheet-metal cornice and the pediments over the windows add interest to what is otherwise a fairly straightforward commercial building. On the ground floor is the jewel of the surviving coffee shops of Hastings Street: the Ovaltine Cafe.

The Ovaltine opened in 1942, succeeding the Blue Eagle and The Eatmor cafes which occupied the space after Burlington Tailors closed up shop in 1940. Inside, the cafe has survived intact with its popular coffee counter—a good place to pick up tips for the track or get the results. On the other side of the central service area there is booth service. The varnished woodwork and mirrors contribute to the atmosphere. The Jersey Farms neon clock remains in place on the back wall above the kitchen entrance, through which you can see the massive freezers. You can also enter the Ovaltine through the kitchen from the lane doorway, often used by police department staff who work just behind the restaurant.

The Ovaltine serves basic coffee-shop fare: pies, burgers, coffee, and so on, with one addition—a west-coast treat—the oolichan.

Coastal natives relied on this fish as a food source but also put it to many other uses. By boiling the fish, they got an oil that was used in cooking, as a remedy for skin burns and in lamps. From this last use came the nickname candle fish.

The Ovaltine's exterior is extra special because of the impact of the neon signage. The window signs, the projecting sign and the sign over the door are all complete. In restaurants elsewhere, the window neon is the first to get damaged and discarded; then the sign over the door is replaced by a backlit plastic one, to modernize the appearance of the business; finally, the large projecting sign is taken down because it is too expensive to maintain. Yet, at the Ovaltine, it all survives today, and with luck there will be no attempt to alter this unique example of 1940s commercial architecture.

Take time to enjoy coffee and pie here at the counter before heading home or walking the few blocks east to the start of the Strathcona tour.

Nelson Park

¹/₂ HOUR

L ike the Delamont Park houses in Kitsilano (Chapter Five), the block of houses south of Nelson Park in the West End is owned by the city, and has been held with the understanding that eventually the land will become open space. Whether the houses are demolished for that purpose, whether they will be restored *in situ* as a heritage park, or whether they will simply fall down due to lack of maintenance is a complex issue whose resolution is dependent on city budgets, trade-offs between City Council and the Park Board, and the political will necessary to effect any change. (The City of Vancouver owns nearly all of the houses facing onto Comox and Pendrell, and a few of the lots facing Bute and Thurlow; it does not own Strathmore Apartments, the largest building on the site.)

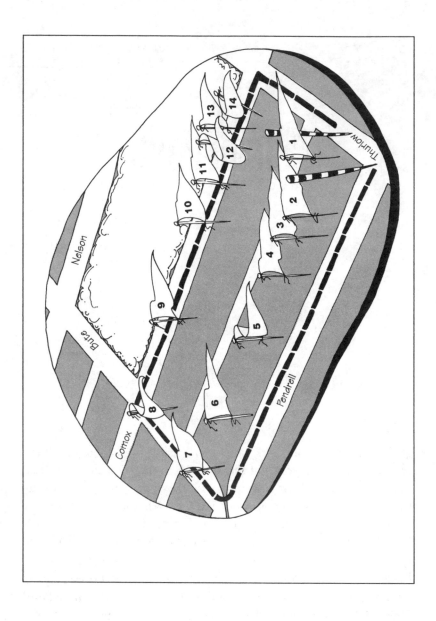

The creation of a heritage park on the block bounded by Thurlow, Pendrell, Bute and Comox (technically, on Block 23 of District Lot 185—Nelson Park itself is the block to the north, between Comox and Nelson) would not be a leap into the unknown for the city: in the 1980s, the Park Board took a chance with Parksite 19 on the block bounded by Barclay, Nicola, Haro and Broughton. Parksite 19 was to have been cleared of buildings, but after years of persistent lobbying by community groups, especially the Community Arts Council of Vancouver, the Park Board decided to preserve several of the historic houses; the result was Barclay Heritage Square, which has proved that functioning buildings and recreational space can coexist.

The Nelson Park houses are, if anything, even more interesting than the restored houses on Barclay Heritage Square. The block was substantially developed over the twenty years from about 1890 to 1910, and contains within it examples of all the middle-class housing styles built in the heyday of the West End. Given that this is the last intact period grouping of houses in this very old Vancouver neighbourhood, it is extraordinary that it should be such a diverse one in both its architecture and history.

The West End in 1890 had only scattered settlement, as it was a long way from the old Granville Townsite (Gastown) which was then the centre of the city. Loggers were gradually pushing the line of forest back towards Stanley Park, and had cleared the land about as far west as Nicola Street. That year, a number of families built houses along Haro and Barclay streets in the blocks just to the west of Burrard Street, which prompted the construction in 1892 of a public school at the corner of Burrard and Barclay. Called the West End School to distinguish it from the Central School (immediately south of Victory Square) and the East End School (now Strathcona Elementary), it inadvertently gave its name to the entire district. Burrard Street extended only as far south as about Comox Street, past which a trail meandered in a roughly southerly direction towards the mouth of False Creek; another trail headed westward from the Comox and Burrard vicinity to the English Bay summer-camping area. The first settler on Comox Street was actually a retiree—Henry Mole, who had been farming the land that is now Point Grey Golf Course since 1862 and decided, in 1889, to move to the fledgling city and build a house just west of Burrard on the north side of

the street. Mole picked the location because it offered him a clear view
to the south, and probably also because he was able to procure running
water from the city's brand new Capilano Reservoir water system.

As settlement of the West End pushed southward towards False
Creek, it linked up with the old Yaletown residential area on the slope
south of Davie Street, dating from the late 1880s when the Canadian
Pacific Railway established its roundhouse and freight yards on the False
Creek flats. The first St. Paul's Hospital, a turreted wooden building on
Burrard Street at Comox, was erected in 1894. Modern transportation
began in the summer of 1890, when Vancouver's first street-railway
system commenced service with a line connecting Granville Street at
Pacific with the well-established city at Hastings and Main. A streetcar
line along Robson Street, laid in 1895, opened up that part of the West
End to settlement; four years later, a new line along Denman Street to
English Bay was completed. Finally, in 1900, the B.C. Electric Railway
Company laid streetcar lines along Davie Street from Granville to
Denman, completing the ring of transit lines around the West End
which is still operational today.

Settlement on the block between Comox and Pendrell west of
Thurlow actually began about 1891, with the construction of a house
on the site of the Strathmore Lodge at Bute and Comox. The water-
permit application in the City Archives records that the owner, whose
signature is illegible, wished to use city water for both a water closet and
a horse, as well as for "domestic purposes" such as drinking and
washing. Although no other information about this first house survives,
it is a good guess that it was a simple, boxy, quite vertical building, with
a stable behind it and possibly a shed for a carriage or cart, and that the
owner used a combination of his feet and his horse to go about his business. The shopping street at that point in the city's history was Cordova
in today's Gastown; it was a long hike while carrying groceries, but most
stores delivered, as did the ice man and the coal-and-sawdust company.

**Start at the corner of Thurlow and Pendrell, and walk west,
circumambulating the block in a clockwise fashion.**

The four houses on Thurlow Street, just to the north of Pendrell,
have been so mangled with stucco and cheap renovations over the

years that it is difficult to see that the houses were originally two identical pairs **(1)**. Like the Smith houses facing Bute Street at the other end of the block, these four houses were built in the summer of 1903 on the subdivided quarters of a single city lot by one person—in this case, a physician named R.C. Boyle, who had his office at Robson and Thurlow and was evidently doing a little speculative development. From the corner of Pendrell and Thurlow, you can see the vacant lot to the north of the lane, which was the site of an interesting 1907 building, the Thurlow Apartments, which was designed like an overgrown house, with a hipped roof and dormers. (Apartment-building design in the city changed radically the following year with the construction of the Manhattan, at Thurlow and Robson. It was a flat-roofed, bay-windowed building with internal light-wells—a more urban form of design.) The vacant lot was briefly the site of Vancouver's heritage mobile home, the Watson house, now located a couple of doors to the west along Pendrell Street.

The Watson house, at 1125 Pendrell just to the west of a much-altered and undistinguished 1907 dwelling, started its life in 1897 at 909 Thurlow Street, a few blocks to the north **(2)**. It is a very good

1. *The houses built by R.C. Boyle in 1903 on Thurlow Street north of Pendrell.*

2. The Watson house, restored at 1125 Pendrell.

example of what happened to house-building styles at the end of the nineteenth century, and is probably best described as a Queen Anne, as is the Bethune house at 1173 Pendrell. The Queen Anne style became an amalgam of all of the Victorian-era house styles of the last half of the century, beginning with the Cottage (in the broad front porch) and the Carpenter Gothic (in the asymmetrical plan and ornamental brackets), adding to it elements of the American Federal style (the pediment over the entranceway) and the Stick style (the framed panels with diagonal board siding underneath the two-storey bay window on the side); the house itself was sheathed in readily available drop siding. It lacks the profusion of scroll-sawn woodwork and decorative shingles typical of other houses of the period, perhaps because the builder, or Mr. Watson, the original owner, wanted a more stately, formal home.

After the property on which it stood was sold for an apartment development, the Watson house was given to the city for a dollar and moved up the street to the vacant lot at Comox and Thurlow; however, no one could decide whether that was a good location for it, so after some time on that site it was moved again, around the corner, and finally placed onto a new foundation and properly restored. Its resting place had once been occupied by a 1904 house, since demolished, built for one D. Robinson, who was a melter in the assay office.

To the west of the Watson house, at 1127 Pendrell, is the 1905 house of James Gillett **(3)**. Although a simple, boxy house, with a hipped roof, bellcast eaves and cyclops dormer, it and the thousands like it that used to line streets in the West End are given a certain grace due to the regular horizontal lines of the shiplap siding, the fine proportions of windows and walls, and the slender columns in groups of two and three supporting the porch. In Vancouver, this type of house is described as an Edwardian Builder or, more simply, as a Vancouver Box—the builder's preferred house design of the early years of the century. In the United States, this type of house with a front porch and cyclops dormer on a hipped roof is usually described as being part of the Georgian Revival Vernacular, the builder's version of the updated colonial Georgian style initiated by McKim, Mead and White in the eastern United States in the 1890s.

Farther along Pendrell Street is a restorable Queen Anne house at 1129-31, built in 1899 for a broker named J.E. Evans. Its original neighbour to the west, on the site of the modern daycare structure, was connected to the city water system a week earlier—so it was probably an identical house by the same builder. Much more significant, because of their age and their condition, are the two classic Queen Annes to the west, at 1137 and 1139 Pendrell **(4)**. Both were completed in the spring of 1893 by an unknown builder. They have the

3. The 1905 Gillett house, a classic West End shoebox, at 1127 Pendrell.

4. The two Queen Annes, built in 1893, at 1137 and 1139 Pendrell.

asymmetrical facades, decorative shingling "feathers" or "fishscales," and scroll-sawn brackets between the eaves and the bay windows typical of that period; if its roof were flat, the house at 1139 would fit perfectly into a San Francisco streetscape. These are the two oldest houses on the block; at nearly one hundred years of age, they are among the oldest half-dozen houses in the entire city.

The house to the west, at 1147 Pendrell, is one of the few on the block to have been built on an entire city lot—most of the others are on half-lots. What remains of the original house is best seen from the back lane, as the front has been modified with a large, apartment-building excrescence, probably from the 1930s or 1940s. The old part dates to 1898, and was built as the residence of Baron de St. Laurent, the French consul in Vancouver at that period.

The four houses numbered 1157, 1159, 1163 and 1169 are all Queen Annes, with double-storey bay windows set off-centre, front stoops and elaborate fretwork detailing and shingling **(5)**. All were built late in 1898, probably by the developer Alex Bethune. Bethune definitely built 1157 and 1159; because of the stylistic similarities of the four, and the fact that they were completed within a few months of each other, it is likely that Bethune was responsible for all of them.

5. 1159 Pendrell, one of four Queen Annes probably built in 1898 by Alex Bethune.

Water-permit applications for some of the houses have been lost, and early city directory information is unclear on the matter of house-numbering, while land-titles information is sketchy and building permits for that period of the city no longer exist. Number 1157 has a square-fronted apartment carbuncle on its front, but is an intact old house behind the stick-on facade, and appears to have been identical with its immediate neighbour to the west.

The big house at 1173 Pendrell was built in 1898 and is a good example of how, in Vancouver, the Carpenter Gothic style of the mid-nineteenth century became softened and adapted to local conditions and materials (6). The house has the kind of informal, rambling floor plan of Carpenter Gothic buildings around North America and a very fine wooden sunburst in the gable—one of a myriad of carpenter-created designs in that period based on anything from the natural world and mass-produced by the steam-powered scroll saw. The house was built by William A. Bauer for a relative, A.M. Bauer; the former was an Australian emigrant of German background who had arrived in

6. 1169 Pendrell, on the right, and 1173 Pendrell.

Vancouver in 1891 and subsequently married Ruby Springer, the daughter of a long-time manager of the Moodyville Sawmill and niece of pioneer Jonathan Miller. "Billy" Bauer, who changed his name to Bower during the First World War, built a number of land-marks in Vancouver, including the Pemberton Building, originally called the Bauer Building, at 744 West Hastings Street.

In 1901, the Bauers moved out and 1173 Pendrell was taken over by the businessman and investor Alex Bethune, who was then at the midpoint of his local political career. Bethune had been born in Peterborough in 1852, followed the railway boom west in the 1880s into Manitoba, then moved to Vancouver in 1891. He was a city alderman in 1894-5 and 1897, again in 1902-3 and 1905-6, and served as mayor in 1907-8. Bethune had a variety of business pursuits, and in some city directories is listed as a builder. He eventually moved to Hollywood, where he died in the 1920s.

The last lot on the block, at the northeast corner of Bute and Pendrell, holds four buildings, the southernmost three of which are identical **(7)**. The fourth building, which now stands at 1104 Bute, was probably built in 1893 facing Pendrell, at which time it occupied the entire lot with a stable in its backyard. It was probably moved in

7. *The Smith houses on Bute Street, with Strathmore Apartments in the background.*

1908 to make room for the three identical buildings which were erected at 1110, 1116 and 1122 Bute. The owner of the property and original occupant was Percy N. Smith, the president of the B.C. Leather Company, who in 1908 was the developer of the three large builders' houses. The original 1893 house is now hidden behind a stucco apartment facade, but its roof peak and side bay window are still visible.

As mentioned above, there existed, in the years before the Strathmore Apartments were erected in 1909, an 1891 house at the southeast corner of Comox and Bute. The Strathmore is one of the great early apartment buildings of the West End—stately and commodious, a forerunner of elegant buildings such as the Beaufort, the Queen Charlotte, the Kensington, and Tudor Manor, which sought to provide an alternative to the tribulations of home ownership for people who still wanted to live in a gracious manner **(8)**.

In the shadow of the Strathmore on Comox Street is a little stucco box, built in the 1940s at number 1178, next door to an 1898 house built probably by Edward Hobson at number 1170. As the original house at 1178 Comox was also evidently by Hobson, on the other half of lot 9, and was completed and connected to the city water

8. The 1909 Strathmore Apartments on Bute Street, undergoing a renovation, probably following a fire, in the mid-1920s. The photograph was taken as part of the Harland Bartholomew city-plan report of 1927, which sought to demonstrate that buildings such as this one, which covered their entire site, were examples of "too intensive property use" (the report lauded Tudor Manor on Beach Avenue as "an apartment conforming with the zoning regulations"). Note the 1893 Smith house, visible immediately to the right of the apartment building, as it appeared before it was modified with a stucco carbuncle on its facade. (W.J. Moore photo, John Atkin collection)

system on the same day, it is reasonable to assume that the two houses were identical. The surviving house at 1170 Comox is one of the earliest houses in the city to be built in a symmetrical, almost classical fashion—a move away from the picturesque, asymmetrical Queen Anne and Carpenter Gothic buildings of the preceding forty years.

Frank Bowser built the house next door, at 1164 Comox Street, in 1895. By comparison with the upright "town" houses in Queen Anne and Builders' styles nearby, Bowser's looks like a farmhouse, with its expansive, wraparound front porch. Bowser was a customs agent who, after about ten years in this house, moved to Kerrisdale and went into property development and local politics; although his ten-acre estate at the corner of Macdonald and 44th Avenue is long gone, the brick Bowser Building, at the corner of 41st and West Boulevard, still defines the entry into the Kerrisdale "village." Bowser's brother William, nicknamed "The Little Napoleon" for the discipline he enforced on the B.C. Conservative Party, was provincial attorney general after 1907, minister of finance after 1909, and premier of the province for most of 1916, before becoming mired in by-election, Dominion Trust, and PGE railway scandals. He continued on as leader of the Conservative party for many years, and eventually died during the 1933 election campaign while running for the legislature as an independent non-partisan.

Even older than the Bowser house is the one to its east at 1160 Comox, built for himself by the carpenter and contractor W.A. Mace in 1893 **(9)**. There was originally a stable in the backyard, and the front porch was added to the original building, probably about 1910. It is likely that Mace worked out the design himself, which has some

9. The upper, original storey of the 1893 Mace house at 1160 Comox.

features from the Stick style popular after about 1865, especially the simple fretwork in the main gable, the two square bays on the upper storey and the horizontal band above them—plus some Carpenter Gothic flourishes like the fishscale shingles, floral brackets and the sunbursts above the upper window.

The house next to Mace's was probably built as a rooming house, rather than being a conversion *into* a rooming-house, in 1906—a time when the character of this part of the West End had evolved from single-family into rooms and suites and small apartments—by a Mr. Rummell. It is, like the Thurlow Apartments that were built the following year at the end of the block, an overgrown house rather than an apartment building in the sense that the latter term is used today. The two houses to the east, at 1150 and 1146 Comox, were built in 1904 and 1905 respectively; both have been stuccoed and stylistically mutilated, but are worth a second look for the wooden sunburst in the gable and the extraordinary turret (probably originally an open-to-the-air breakfast balcony) at the rear of 1150, and the asymmetrical Queen Anne turret blanketed in stucco blandness on 1146.

Numbers 1136 and 1140 Comox are almost identical houses, but were apparently built a decade apart, although by the same carpenter, Francis Curry **(10)**. The earlier one is 1136, which was completed in 1897, making it a very early example of the symmetrical builders' houses—the "Vancouver Specials" of the period—that were the

10. The two houses built in 1897 and 1907 by Francis Curry.

design of choice until the Craftsman style became popular around 1912. It is worth comparing these houses with the other Vancouver Boxes on the block—the Hobson house at 1170, built in 1898; and the Gillett house at 1127 Pendrell, built in 1905—to see the variations and evolution of this vernacular style. The Parr and Fee houses at 1120 and 1122 Comox are slightly later and more elaborate versions of the Curry houses.

The vacant lot next door dates only to 1991, and a decision by the city's director of permits and licenses that the 1895 house on the site was uninhabitable and a public nuisance; its demolition revived the debate about the future of Nelson Park alluded to below. The house at 1126 Comox—the second-newest one on the block, having been built in the 1920s—is the only house on this block of Comox Street not owned by the city (the owner apparently has refused to sell); note its extraordinary carved dragon-head bargeboards.

The two Edwardian Builder houses at 1122 and 1120 Comox seem at first glance to be mirror images of each other, but differ in their porch columns and the detailing of the gable. Both were completed early in 1904 by the speculative builder Stanley Judson Steeves, who had commissioned the well-known and highly productive architectural firm of Parr and Fee to design a house (number 1122) **(11)**, which he then altered slightly to build 1120 **(12)**. Both houses have the expansive, solid wood feeling of the best of the old West End— very large porch posts, wide porches, substantial bay windows into which a decent-sized table and a couple of overstuffed chairs could fit, all in a tall package fitted neatly onto a narrow lot. The three speculatively built Smith houses on Bute Street, although slightly different in design, have that same massiveness.

The last two houses on the block are both Queen Annes, built about 1906, for a merchant named James Tomlinson (1114 Comox) **(13)** and a broker named Sam Castleman (1110) **(14)**. Both have slender, round, grouped columns holding up their front porches and rather formal little pediments above staircases at right angles to the facades. Above the main floor, however, any formality disappears in a jumble of turrets and dormers and bellcast rooflines—a riotous example of the carpenter-built vernacular architecture of turn-of-the-century Vancouver. Number 1114 has an octagonal turret with a

11. (top, left) *1122 Comox, designed in 1904 by Parr and Fee.*
12. (top, right) *The copycat 1120 Comox, built at the same time as
1122 Comox by S.J. Steeves.*
13. (bottom, left) *The Queen Anne-style Tomlinson house, at 1114 Comox.*
14. (bottom, right) *The Castleman house, with its odd, flat-roofed turret.*

bellcast roof, whereas the square, diagonally set turret or stair tower (reminiscent of a silo) on 1110 looks as if it once had a fancy roof, but in fact never did—the turret was flat-roofed even around 1915.

Regrettably, these last four houses are not in good condition, and without maintenance are beginning to deteriorate rapidly. In the spring of 1991, the pending loss of these houses and the bulldozing of the house at 1132-4 Comox brought the issue of Nelson Park back into sharp focus.

To attempt to find a solution, the Park Board had in 1986 commissioned the Coriolis Consulting group to study the block. The consultants developed three proposals: an all-park option, involving the demolition of almost everything on the block and the creation of "active" park space such as tennis courts and a playing field; an all-housing option, involving the restoration of the heritage houses and the replacement of non-heritage buildings with new apartments; and a compromise option, involving the relocation of heritage houses from Comox Street to vacant lots on Pendrell Street and the development of the Comox Street side of the block for "active" park uses.

This third option, which would create a manufactured heritage streetscape on Pendrell Street, completely ignores the concept of "spirit of place." Unfortunately, it appeared in 1991 to be the favourite choice of the Park Board.

A potential heritage area such as this has two strengths—its architecture and its history. If the houses are moved, all that is left is the architecture. The result of this kind of approach is to create an architectural petting zoo, a kind of heritage-mobile-home park, like the much-ridiculed Heritage Square in Los Angeles. It is not a contradiction to say that the relocation of the Watson House onto Pendrell Street was a sensible move under the circumstances of the late 1980s—it had to go somewhere, and the lot on Pendrell was already vacant.

A better plan would be to restore the heritage houses on their sites, and to consider removing a few of the non-heritage, badly deteriorated and severely altered houses along both Comox and Pendrell in order to create mini-parks—heritage "vacant lots," as it were. If public money were nowhere to be found, the houses could be designated and sold to private interests who had demonstrated their ability to restore them; they could be restored as family housing or might become offices or condos, subtly fenced off from the miniparks and walkways. A positive aspect of this plan is the fact that it would be possible to do slowly and incrementally, as money comes available, beginning with the restoration of the four houses at the east end of Comox Street, which have great heritage value yet are seriously run down. A slow, thoughtful redevelopment of the block would also avoid a callous en masse uprooting of tenants, and could allow the design of infill mini-parks to develop gradually and sensitively. It is a golden opportunity to create something distinctive in the midst of the towers and hustle-bustle of the modern West End.

Grandview

1 ½ HOURS

It was not a local streetcar line, but an interurban line connecting Vancouver with New Westminster, that opened Grandview to settlement. In 1891, when the area was just bush, far to the east of the built-up sections of infant Vancouver (although within the city limits), a syndicate of local businessmen decided to put together a transit system to link the two significant coastal mainland cities of British Columbia, and invested in the recently invented technology of the electric railway.

The route chosen between the two cities included the rough roadway known as Park Drive, so named because it led from Hastings Street to the parkland given to the city in 1889 by E.J. Clark, on the condition that it be developed and maintained as a public recreation

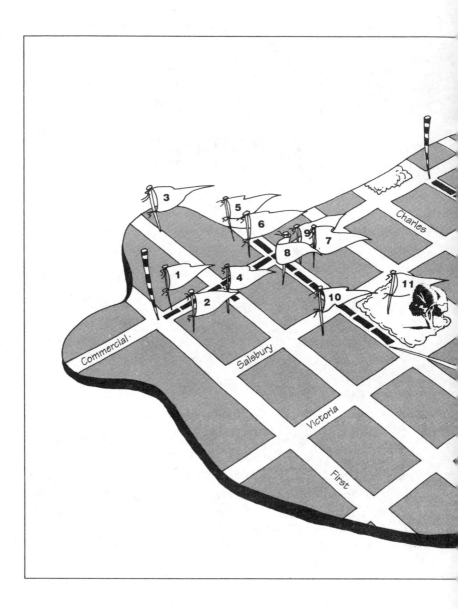

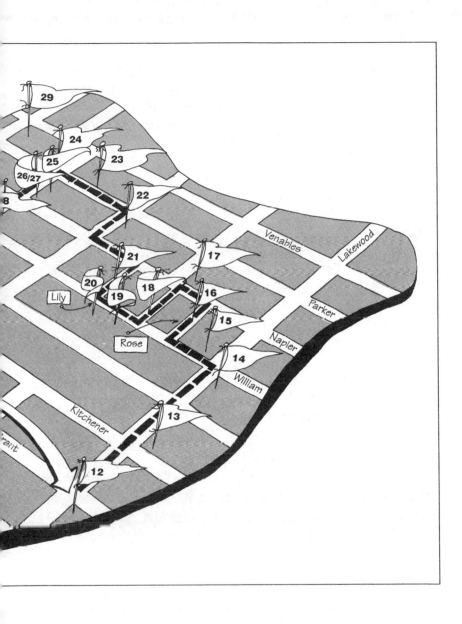

place. At the time of the donation, Clark Park, at what is now 14th and Commercial, was in the middle of nowhere, and twenty years passed before ratepayers in the expanding city petitioned City Hall for improvements to the land. In 1911, the same time that 9th Avenue became Broadway, Westminster Avenue became Main Street and Westminster Road became Kingsway, Park Drive became Commercial Drive—in the middle of the boom years that culminated with the First World War—but its great expectations never materialized. It is now known to locals simply as "The Drive."

According to future city archivist Major J.S. Matthews, when he was a cadet in the Duke of Connaught's Own Rifles in the mid-1890s, the regiment used to travel by interurban from downtown Vancouver, along Park Drive and thence through the forested wilderness to the Central Park area where they held their drill and target practices. Matthews recalled seeing the first sign in the area—the word "GRANT" daubed in black paint on a board nailed to a stump at the rough roadway that became Grant Avenue.

There are several conflicting stories about the naming of Grandview. According to Matthews, it was unnamed until about 1893 and, if known at all, was referred to as District Lot 264A. Victoria Drive and Park Drive below Hastings Street were skid roads to move logs to the water at what was then called Cedar Cove, at the end of Victoria Drive on the inlet. One anonymous pioneer story noted by Matthews recounted that an old man named Cronk, "who lived on the corner where Odlum's house is" (Grant Avenue at Commercial), chose the name to call attention to the prospect from his well-placed property. Others claimed that two settlers competed to have the interurban stop named "Smith's Station" or "Grand View." Matthews recalled reading it first in the report of a meeting of local ratepayers, probably the Grandview Progressive Association, and hearing about 1904, that Professor Edward Odlum, one of the significant property owners in the area, had agreed that "Grandview would be an excellent name."

Early settlement was a combination of individuals buying single lots and property syndicates acquiring entire blocks, subdividing them and even on occasion building houses "on spec" to entice development. Although a few hardy settlers ventured into the area in the early

1890s, the real spur to development was the arrival of the city water system along Commercial Drive about 1904, and the establishment of local streetcar service by the B.C. Electric Railway Company. According to a 1936 book by the Templeton School Archivists' Club, the BCER offered a year's free transit to anyone establishing a home in the area. This triggered the kind of real-estate development noted below by firms such as the Grandview Land and Trust Company. The *Province* advertised one especially imaginative promotion in its December 22, 1906, edition: purchasers of property in a subdivision bounded by Venables, Parker, Lakewood and Templeton (slightly to the northeast of the area encompassed by this tour) had a chance of winning two Shetland ponies, a two-seater rig and a brass-mounted harness, with a total value of $700.

A later period of development in East Vancouver was triggered by the completion of the Burnaby Lake interurban line in 1912. This line, officially known as the Fourth District of the BCER's interurban system, had its terminus at 6th and Commercial; the line looped away from the 1891 "Central Park" interurban line, swung to the northeast, then turned due east along the median of 1st Avenue; at the outskirts of the city, the line followed the route of today's Highway 1, before swinging around to the southwest and following Columbia Street into downtown New Westminster. One development prompted by this regular transportation system was Grandview Heights—one of the dozens of "heights" for the "Vancouverheights" of the time, as the saying went—which occupied the land bounded by 5th Avenue, Charles, Nanaimo and Boundary Road. (This land had been part of the old Hastings Townsite, between Nanaimo and Boundary north of 29th Avenue, until amalgamation with the City of Vancouver in 1910. Hastings Townsite had been surveyed in the late 1860s by a Royal Navy crew supervised by Admiral George Fowler Hastings. The portion of Grandview Heights east of Clinton Park had previously been known as Hastings Manor—the stump-strewn estate of the colourful B.C. premier "Fighting Joe" Martin.) Grandview Heights was a promotion of the notorious Alvo von Alvensleben, whose management of German capital in British Columbia in the years before the First World War helped to create one of the largest real-estate booms in western Canadian history; the collapse of that boom, due in part to European war scares and the withdrawal of overseas capital, brought down the Dominion Trust Company, to which von Alvensleben owed millions, and indirectly caused the demise of the Conservative provincial government.

Start at the corner of 1st Avenue and Commercial Drive.

Although the first settlers in Grandview built their little houses among the puddles near 1st Avenue and Commercial Drive in the early 1890s, the actual commercial development of that part of "The Drive" did not commence until about 1909. The little sundries store still sporting a "Star Weekly" sign at 1721 Commercial was connected to the city's water system in May, 1909, by a man named Leon Melakov.

More significant architecturally is the building at the southeast corner of 1st and Commercial, built in 1910 by a contractor named Herbert D. Crawford, who lived not far away at 816 East 12th **(1)**. Although its metal-sheathed bay windows and corner bay are still in their original condition, the pointed metal turret and some of the ground-floor shopfront detailing have disappeared. Early photographs show the building to have had a broad canvas awning sheltering the main-floor shops. Around the First World War years, it was a typical mixed commercial and residential block, with a drygoods shop and a confectioner on the main floor and upstairs tenants. Residents included

1. *Looking south on Commercial Drive to the corner of 1st Avenue in 1922.*
(P. Timms photo, VPL 7399)

the brothers Bagnall—one a physician and the other a dentist—and an artist named Mrs. D.C. Chase.

The building adjoining Crawford's commercial block to the south was originally the Grandview Theatre, which commenced operation early in the silent era, around 1913. To its south, 1714-1716 Commercial was originally known as the Dryden Block, and proclaimed its name in carved letters on a masonry parapet, since lost, above the cornice; it was the home for decades of Manitoba Hardware. The northwest corner of 1st and Commercial was the site of the old Grandview School.

The northeast corner of 1st and Commercial is now home to a drab Bank of Commerce building dating from the 1940s, but was originally the site of a more interesting bank building: a B.C. Mills, Timber and Trading Company prefab. Many of the surviving examples of the BCMT&T's prefabricated, modular building system are in the Grandview area. The Bank of Commerce was a regular purchaser of the BCMT&T's bank buildings; although the one at 1st and Commercial was replaced many years ago, there is still a surviving Bank of Commerce prefab, in a different design, now functioning as the museum at Mission. The Northern Bank was also a BCMT&T customer; its building in Steveston became the museum of the Steveston Historical Society.

Just to the east of Commercial Drive, at 1735 East 1st, there is a another example of a BCMT&T prefab—a Model "OOO" house with a gambrel roof **(2)**, erected there in 1905 as the residence for a carpenter named Thomas Gray. Regrettably, it has been altered quite significantly over the years. The old windows have been replaced by aluminum ones, and the prefab system's distinctive modular wall units have recently been covered by "the vinyl solution."

Walk north on Commercial Drive to Graveley Street.

From the corner of Commercial and Graveley, it is possible to see the site of the first home in Grandview, which stood at 1617 Graveley, on the north side of the street to the west of Commercial Drive, on land now occupied by an apartment building. Built in 1891 or 1892 by L.T. Sankey and Harry Langdale (who could not remember which

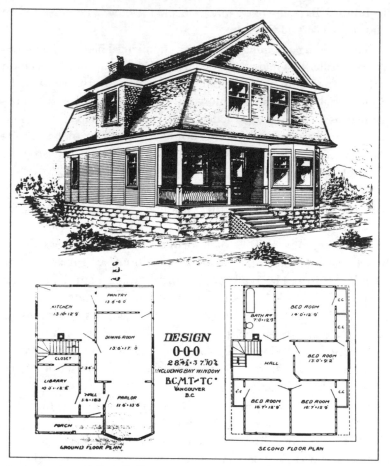

2. A page from the B.C. Mills, Timber and Trading Company's 1906 catalogue, showing a Model "OOO" prefabricated house.

year they built it), the first house in Grandview was a little upright box with side gables and, originally, a tiny pedimented front stoop with scroll-sawed fretwork on its two porch posts **(3)**. Built for John Mason, the fireman at the B.C. Sugar Refinery, and his wife, the house originally had only two rooms, but was later extended with a shed-roofed addition at the rear for kitchen and toilet and a full-width front porch.

According to the Williams B.C. Directory of 1893, the Masons

3. The Mason cottage at 1617 Graveley Street, in the early 1890s.
(Photographer unknown, CVA Bu.P.299)

had only a handful of neighbours, none of whom was on their block. The block to the south was evidently home to four families, while the block to the east contained two, including the above-mentioned B.M. Cronk. One early resident of the area about whom some information has survived is Charles Burns, the foreman for Royal City Mills (part of the BCMT&T); two of his daughters, Jennie May and Marion Alice, were born in 1892 and 1894 respectively in a "smaller house than the present one" at 1732 Kitchener Street—the earlier house having been destroyed by fire.

As for the other early residents, it is impossible to tell exactly where they lived and whether or not the original houses survive today. Directory information for the area is incomplete and inaccurate, perhaps not surprisingly, as Grandview was so far out in the country. In addition, surveys were inaccurate, the early records of the Land Titles Office are incomplete, and land ownership records do not show when buildings were constructed. The best information about the development of the area, other than the oral history and photographs collected in the 1930s and 1940s for the City Archives by J.S. Matthews, comes from the water-connection permits, signed by owners, beginning in this area in 1905.

The oldest building surviving on Graveley Street is probably the John Ross house at number 1744; stylistically, its Carpenter Gothic shape (albeit without the elaborate wooden decoration typical of the style), sweeping porch, and old-fashioned drop siding place it as an 1890s building, although it was connected to the water system in 1906. John Ross signed that permit application, but the first entry in a city directory records the occupant as William Ross, whose occupation in 1908 was listed as shipper.

The other interesting building on this part of Graveley Street is now known as the Grace Chinese Methodist Church, but was built in 1922 as the Grandview Lodge of the International Order of Odd Fellows **(4)**. Fraternal societies such as the IOOF, many of which provided a sort of "safety net" for members in the form of health insurance and death benefits, were common throughout Vancouver and filled the gap between private charity and government indifference to the welfare of individuals. In 1918, shortly before this building's erection, the IOOF was the largest fraternal society in the world, with 1,622,100 members in the United States alone.

Walk north on Commercial Drive to Grant Avenue, and turn west (left).

On the slope below Commercial Drive, at 1636 Grant Avenue, is another very old building whose construction probably predates the

4. The Grandview Lodge of the IOOF, built in 1922 on Graveley Street just east of Commercial Drive.

5. The West house at 1636 Grant Avenue.

arrival of piped water in the area **(5)**. It is a simple little gabled box, clad in drop siding and enlivened by a rather elegant wraparound porch. Its first known resident was Tom West, who in 1905 worked as an "elevator man," presumably meaning that he operated an elevator in one of the very modern office buildings downtown, perhaps the Empire Building at Hastings and Seymour, since demolished, which featured one of the first open-cage elevators in the city.

Even smaller than West's house is the unique BCMT&T prefabricated cottage at 1656 Grant, identifiable as a prefab by its battens **(6)**. It is impossible to tell when this house was put on the site, although it was connected to the water system in 1918 by the local property owner Edward Odlum, whose own considerably larger house is only a few doors away on the other side of Commercial Drive. BCMT&T ceased production of its prefabs in 1910, so it is possible either that the house received running water several years after it was erected on the site, or else that it was moved to the site from somewhere else. It is unique because it is a single-storey gabled cottage; the only other gabled BCMT&T houses in Vancouver are the three prototypes on Hawks Avenue, which have a habitable half-storey under the eaves. The only other known example of this cottage design in the Lower Mainland is the original portion of the Malkin cottage on Bowen Island.

6. The BCMT&T cottage at 1656 Grant.

Cross Commercial Drive and walk east on Grant Avenue.

By comparison with other parts of the city, there is a tremendous range of housing types in Grandview, from shacks to mansions, often sharing the same streets in a free-for-all fashion. Elsewhere in Vancouver, it was not unusual for a neighbourhood to evolve as fortunes faded and times changed and to have small houses infilled onto the grounds of mansions, but Grandview is unique in that cabins were being built at the same time, and on the same streets, as large and elaborate homes. Land use also varied widely from block to block— "Wilga," seen later in this walk, occupied an entire city block, although across the street from it the land was subdivided into three-thousand-square-foot lots for inexpensive builders' houses. On the west side of Vancouver, where the building standards and sizes were set, and enforced by covenant, by major landowners such as the Canadian Pacific Railway, there was much more consistency from block to block and house to house.

Of the buildings surviving on the block of Grant Avenue east of Commercial, the oldest is the very fine bracketed house at 1747 Grant, completed early in 1905 by the contractor H.E. French and best described stylistically as a hybrid of Stick and Shingle styles of the mid to late nineteenth century **(7)**. Although it is a substantial home, it is small compared with the Edward Odlum house across the street at number 1774, which was completed early in 1906 **(8)**. The latter is a good example of the Queen Anne style, with an octagonal corner turret and elegant bellcast eaves. It originally stood on a much bigger piece of property, which was infilled with little stucco bungalows in

7. *The H.E. French house, built in 1905 at 1747 Grant Avenue.*

the 1940s. After years as a rooming house, it was renovated and restored as a cooperative in the 1970s.

Edward Odlum was probably the most historically important early resident of Grandview. Born in Ontario in 1850, he spent his early years in scientific research and was involved in the development of

8. *The Edward Odlum house, "Hillcrest," at 1774 Grant Avenue, about 1910.*
(Photographer unknown, CVA Bu.P.649)

electric light and the telephone. His interest in comparative ethnology took him around the world several times to study peoples as diverse as Australian bushmen and Laplanders, and led him in his later years to a belief that the Anglo-Saxon race was one of the lost tribes of Israel (this so-called British-Israelite theory had wide currency among some scholars in the 1920s and 1930s); in his old age, Odlum was a regular voice on the British-Israelite hour on syndicated radio. In addition, he was actively involved in real-estate development—especially in the Grandview area, where his real-estate office was at 1542 Commercial, barely a block from his house—and in financial management, where his name survives today in the Odlum Brown stockbrokerage. As noted above, he was the owner of the BCMT&T cottage at 1656 Grant; one of his sons owned and lived in another BCMT&T cottage mentioned below; another of his sons, Victor, achieved prominence as a military figure, politician, and newspaperman, and lived for a time in the Logan house near Kitsilano beach.

The two cottages at 1721 and 1723 Grant are at the opposite end of the construction spectrum from Odlum's house **(9)**. Both were built by the carpenter Isaac Russell, whose domicile in the 1908 directory is listed as 1428 Park Drive; it is possible that they predate the turn of the century, although their water permits indicate that they were completed in 1907 (1723 Grant) and 1908 (1721 Grant).

9. The cottages at 1721 and 1723 Grant Avenue.

Both have the quality of Lower Mainland homesteaders' cottages—a simple peaked roofline, a shed-roofed addition at the rear for kitchen and plumbing, and a front porch, much like the Mason cottage mentioned above. In addition, they retain a paint colour best described as "CPR red," which adds to their historic character.

Although the early land-ownership pattern on these blocks is unclear, it is evident that some of the houses near the corner of Salsbury and Grant were built as part of real-estate promotions. The three identical houses at 1505-1523 Salsbury were completed in 1909 for the National Finance Company, one of the many land-development corporations controlled by Thomas Talton Langlois from the B.C. Permanent Loan Company building at 350 West Pender. Langlois's activities in Vancouver before the First World War are best

10. The cottage at 1528 Salsbury, built in 1905 for the Grandview Land and Trust Company.

remembered in the Talton Place subdivision—the blocks of 13th, 14th, 15th and 16th between Cypress and Arbutus. (The spelling of Salsbury is not an incorrect version of the English cathedral-town name; it was named for the CPR treasurer William Ferriman Salsbury, and first appears on a 1902 city map.)

The very fine little cottage at 1528 Salsbury was built in 1905 by another real-estate firm, the Grandview Land and Trust Company, probably as an inducement to further settlement and construction on the block **(10)**. The two principals of this firm, H.M. Fraser and Alex Dow, both lived at Central Park and worked at 307 West Cordova Street in the Gastown area, and so probably passed through Grandview on their way to and from work each day on the interurban. No doubt seeing the potential of the area, they bought some land, subdivided it, and left this white house on Salsbury as their legacy.

Continue eastward along Grant Street.

Note the BCMT&T prefab at 1860 Grant—a design which does not appear in the BCMT&T's surviving catalogue—erected in 1906

11. *The view in 1922 from the hose tower of the fire hall that stood at the corner of Charles and Salsbury, looking south towards Victoria Park. (P. Timms photo, VPL 7424)*

for Edward Faraday Odlum, a block to the east of his father's house. It is the dark house facing the park, visible in the right middle ground of a 1922 photograph **(11)**, and appears to have been altered very little since. If the weather is decent, there will probably be a group of men playing *bocce* in the park across the street. Although this part of Grandview has had a pronounced Italian ambience since after the Second World War (when the Italians migrated eastward from Strathcona), in the years before that it was much more Anglo-Saxon. Directory information from 1925 records several members of the Odlum family on Grant Street, as well as fuel-company president Joseph Dobson at 1747, a physician named Fredrick Dunlop at 1727, and the manager of the Columbia Hotel, N.D. Cameron, in the little cottage at 1528 Salsbury.

Turn north (left) at Lakewood Drive.

At the crest of the hill, where Grant Street meets Lakewood Drive, there is a turreted Queen Anne built early in 1909 by the contractor James Ball for himself **(12)**. Ball was one of a number of carpenter/ contractors who both lived and built houses in the area.

12. *The Queen Anne-style Ball house at the corner of Lakewood and Grant.*

13. The Foster house at 2111 Kitchener.

A block to the north of Grant is Kitchener Street, renamed about 1915 from Bismarck Street, much as Berlin, Ontario, became Kitchener. At 2111 Kitchener, on the corner of Kitchener and Lakewood, is perhaps the rarest house style in the Grandview area, a very fine Georgian Revival building from 1931, built for Dr. Edwin Foster, who had his practice on East Hastings near Nanaimo, and his wife, Etheluna **(13)**. These houses are very common in the southern parts of Shaughnessy and in Kerrisdale, where they often sit on comparatively parklike properties, but this Grandview example is jammed onto a small lot, with its roofline almost touching the house behind.

The almost-identical row of eight houses on Lakewood Drive between William and Charles is the type of consistent streetscape that, because of the ups and downs of the local economy and the independent, underfinanced nature of most early contractors, is rare in Vancouver. Although in a different style, these eight are reminiscent of the rows of Craftsman houses and California Bungalows in Kitsilano. The main design feature of the eight houses—the strongly triangular front gable—remains fairly consistent throughout the row, although each differs subtly from its neighbour.

The southernmost four of the eight-house row were built in 1910 by the above-mentioned James Ball. Like their neighbours to the north, they were subtly different from each other while retaining a consistent style. Regrettably, on all but one of the eight houses on the block, most of the original detail has disappeared in the eight decades since their construction, and today the houses are to varying degrees disfigured by stucco, enclosed porches, and poor-quality windows.

The four northernmost houses were built in 1909 by a carpenter named Storer J. Wing, aka Chin Wing, who was living at 1570 Bismarck at the time but who moved into 1204 Lakewood in 1910. The latter house, with its river-stone porch piers, half-timbering in the gable, and the peaked-roof dormer on the north side, is more elaborate than the other three, which have shed dormers on the sides and wooden porch posts. All were originally shingle-covered with arched spans between the porch posts and above the upstairs sleeping porches, as in the Shingle-style builders' houses of the Eastern United States; the three houses to the south of Chin Wing's own house orig-inally had little decorative shingles cut as mock-keystones at the cen-tres of the arches (today they survive only on number 1210).

The one survivor which is in its original condition—and can claim to be the least-altered heritage house in the entire city—is the Evelyn Harris house at 1210 Lakewood, owned by the same family since 1919 **(14)**. It has not needed restoration as it was never allowed to deteriorate.

14. The Harris house, built in 1909 at 1210 Lakewood Drive.

Turn west (left) on William Street, then north (right) on Rose Street.

The next several blocks through which you pass are among the most interesting in the city because of the different types of houses, ranging from cottage to mansion, and the intimate sense of community which seems to cling to the short streets and gardens and narrow sidewalks. Like parts of the West End, it is an area that seems to be closed in upon itself, without the long views and sight lines down streets and towards distant mountains and rooftops that seem so typical of other areas, including even the blocks of Grandview immediately adjoining these.

Rose and Lily streets appear to have been subdivisions effected in 1908 or 1909 on the blocks of land between the older Victoria Drive, Semlin, and Lakewood streets, ironically inserting some of the more dense single-family housing in the city onto small lots cheek by jowl with the large, well-landscaped properties along Napier and Victoria Drive. Lily Street first appears in the 1912 city directory, spelled "Lilly." No one knows where the names came from, but it is likely that, as was often the case in the Cedar Cottage and Mount Pleasant neighbourhoods, they were named for relatives of the subdivider.

15. The two houses at 2061 and 2065 William.

Two pairs of houses on William Street between Lakewood and Rose were built speculatively. The two with Juliet balconies at 2061 and 2065 William were commissioned in 1909 by a speculator named James Laird Northey **(15)**. He had been a shipper for the large hardware firm McLennan, McFeely and Company until that year, when he went into real estate with Walter J. Thomas as Northey, Thomas and Company. More modest are the two identical, plain boxes at 2050 and 2058 William, built in 1908 by the contractor J.A. Chisholm.

Rose Street is one-sided—that is, the houses, all of which are on twenty-five- by ninety-six-foot lots, line its east side, while on the west side are the back fences of Semlin Street houses. Furthering the neighbourhood feeling of this intimate little block are the funky signs tacked to lamp posts, cautioning motorists to respect the feline rights-of-way, and so on. Of the Rose Street houses, numbers 1132, 1122 and 1118 were all completed in September, 1909, by the above-mentioned carpenter Chin Wing. Another local speculator, J. Lennox Wilson, built 1112 Rose Street early in 1910 **(16)**. Not surprisingly, due to the short lots and modest houses, Rose Street became home to people of comparatively modest means: a postal clerk named C. Felix in 1112, and a trackman, a construction company foreman, and a sheet-metal worker in other houses during the 1920s.

Turn west (left) on Napier, then south (left) on Semlin.

Contrast these modest houses with the brick assemblage at Napier Street now occupied by the Franciscan Church and friary. Although it has been church property for about seventy years, and infilled since by the small houses lining Semlin and Napier streets, it was originally

16. Rose Street houses.

17. *"Wilga," at 1020 Semlin Street.*

a private estate occupying the entire block—just under two-and-one-half acres with trails, gardens, a tennis court, a stable, and the large house called "Wilga" at 1020 Semlin Street **(17)**. Designed in 1908 by the architects Beam and Brown, "Wilga" was built for William Miller, one of four brothers who moved to Vancouver from Australia in 1905. William and his brother John ("J.J.") both settled in Grandview and were briefly very wealthy, the legacy of which is the massive houses "Wilga" and "Kurrajong."

The Miller family were originally from Dorset, England, but immigrated to New South Wales in the mid-nineteenth century and settled in the graziers' town of Cootamundra. There the family established a sheep station called "Littledale" and became well known as stock agents. Five sons were born, beginning in 1860 with J.J., who at the age of thirty became mayor of Cootamundra. However, following a terrible drought in 1902-1904, the family decided that the station could only support one of the sons, so J.J., William, Alexander and Compton boarded the *Aorangi* for Vancouver, arriving after a stormy crossing, steerage-class, on March 17, 1905. The fifth brother, Neville, stayed in Cootamundra and ultimately was the most successful.

The two elder brothers, J.J. and William, had a flair for real estate and auctioneering, and arrived in Vancouver in the early years of a tremendous real-estate boom. Within a few years, both were very rich; a story survives of a single-day auction of $1,250,000 worth of Prince Rupert town lots, conducted by J.J. in anticipation of the arrival there of the Grand Trunk Pacific Railway. J.J. Miller built "Kurrajong," naming it for a shrubby tree in eastern Australia valuable as fodder during periods of drought, on Salsbury Drive (the walking tour passes it a few blocks farther along); William Miller built "Wilga," naming it for a shrub that has the same use as the kurrajong.

Of the brothers, the most civic-minded was J.J., a self-important man, fond of responsibility and his position in society and as the eldest of the family—he styled his clothing, beard and mannerisms after those of Edward VII. Before he set out for Vancouver, he had duly considered the value of a spouse and so married the widowed mother-in-law of two of his brothers, assuming responsibility for her six unmarried daughters. A highlight of his life was his trip to London to represent Vancouver at the coronation of George V in 1911; upon his return, he published his self-aggrandizing reminiscences as *Vancouver to the Coronation*, copies of which can occasionally be found in antique bookshops.

More importantly, J.J. Miller retained his interest in the improvement of stock to the extent of organizing a local exhibition along the lines of the New South Wales agricultural fairs with which he had been so involved in the 1890s. He negotiated the civic lease of Hastings Park, and the country fair there evolved into the Pacific National Exhibition. Miller Drive on the PNE grounds is named for him.

Both J.J. and William lost their fortunes in the real-estate crash that immediately preceded the First World War. After the war, J.J. gave up "Kurrajong" and lived in a series of rental houses in North Vancouver and Hastings Townsite, before settling at 2331 Graveley Street. He lived until 1950. William hung onto "Wilga" until the 1920s, then lived in a series of rented houses in East Vancouver before moving in 1936 to Berkeley, California, where he lived with a daughter until his death in 1944. Both brothers would have been destitute without their children's largesse.

Although "Wilga" has been greatly altered and has lost much of its detailing, including the gable screens, terracotta ridge cresting in the Australian Federation style, and wraparound front porch with grouped columns, it remains an imposing house. Still visible are the precast concrete balusters on the two entrance staircases and fence, and the precast, rusticated concrete blocks that form the cornerposts for the fence and the supporting walls for the staircases.

Concrete blocks, being a manufactured stone, were used in a surprising number of houses in British Columbia. Many of the local ones were Bond-O-Steel blocks and were manufactured by the Victor Cement Block and Machine Company, which held the patent for a process invented by Mr. A. Crisp, manager of the Vancouver Construction Company. By 1907, the Victor Company—which claimed worldwide rights for the process—claimed some twenty-eight houses had been built using Bond-O-Steel blocks. Concrete-block houses are surprisingly common in the old parts of British Columbia towns, including Chilliwack and Revelstoke.

Across the street from "Wilga," at 1976 Napier, is the home of J. Lennox Wilson, mentioned above for the house on Rose Street which he evidently had built as a speculation. Wilson was obviously not a real-estate developer or agent in the same league as William Miller, as he apparently never quit his day job as a commercial agent; instead, he dabbled in house building and sales during the boom years before the First World War. His own little house, which was probably quite picturesque and decorated with gingerbread in its heyday, is unusual for the square turret offset from what is otherwise a simple hipped-roof box. Possibly the turret started off life as what was often called a breakfast balcony—a sort of attached pergola—that would have permitted Wilson a pleasant view across to the grandeur of his neighbour's estate. In the mid-twenties, the house at 1954 Napier, next door to Wilson's, was home to the Italian consul, Nicolas Masi, his wife, Catherine, and daughter, Josephine, who worked as a seamstress at Shaughnessy Heights Drapery on Granville Street.

Semlin Street, named for the hapless B.C. premier Charles Augustus Semlin, has a land-use pattern as chaotic and interesting as were B.C. politics during Semlin's time. (Semlin became premier following the dismissal of his predecessor, but had a difficult time controlling the vicious infighting in his caucus; following a year of constant interference by the lieutenant-governor, he himself was dismissed on February 27,

18. The Semlin Grocery, one of Vancouver's increasingly rare mid-block grocery stores. The photograph looks north, with "Wilga" and the tower of the Franciscan church visible in the background.

1900, ushering in the forty-day regime of "Fighting Joe" Martin.) This block of Semlin Street between Napier and William has one of the few mid-block grocery stores left in Vancouver, in operation since about 1920, with Mrs. Smith—probably a widow—as the grocer in the early years **(18)**. The oldest building on the block is the much-altered rooming house at 1170 Semlin, finished late in 1906 and interesting because its water-permit application notes that the building was to be used for two families and two roomers. This is such a contrast with "Wilga," which was built down the street a few years later, and reverses the usual Vancouver pattern, seen on Seaton Street (now West Hastings), the West End, and Shaughnessy Heights, where elegant and exclusive single-family homes preceded apartment conversions and tenants.

Turn west (right) on William, north (right) on Lily, and finally west (left) on Napier to Victoria Drive.

Just to the west of the junction of Semlin and William, at 1992 William, there is a new house designed by and for Tom and Megan Otton and completed in 1992 **(19)**. It manages to fit into the style of the neighbourhood, make good use of its twenty-five-foot lot, and yet not be derivative of the styles of the old houses; the one anomaly is the garage on the front, which was required by the city, ostensibly because there is no back lane.

To the west of the Otton house are two tall Queen Anne houses on twenty-five-foot lots, at 1970 and 1972 William; originally identical, they were finished in the summer of 1909 by a carpenter named J. Gruning. The facade of 1972 William is still intact **(20)**, while that of 1970 William has been unsympathetically modernized, destroying much of its charm. This style of house was common in the West End (a few very similar houses from 1898 survive on Pendrell Street; see Chapter Three) and Strathcona (such as the 1898 house at 630 Princess Street) several years before these two were built.

Lily Street, like Rose Street, is an infill between older streets; the properties on the west side are all ninety feet deep, while those on the east are one hundred and five feet deep, somewhat shallower than typical single-family lot depths elsewhere in the East End. All of the buildings on the west side were built in 1910 by a contractor named A. McLellan, who lived near 8th and Commercial. The most interesting house on the east side of the street is 1138 Lily, which was probably

19. (left) *The Otton house at 1992 William, under construction in the summer of 1992.*
20. (right) *The more-intact of the two Queen Anne-style Gruning houses, at 1972 William Street.*

erected late in 1906 by a builder named R.W. Beach. By the look of it, its front door originally faced Napier Street, although its water-permit application indicates that its address was originally a William Street one **(21)**. Note how the house appears to have been modified to change its entrance; possibly, it sat alone on the block for a few years along with a few cows and a farmyard before the eastward march of the city overtook it and the owner subdivided the block into little lots.

One of the finer houses built on the block is the Craftsman home at the southeast corner of Lily and Napier. There are only scattered examples of the Craftsman style in Grandview, where even as late as 1910 the preferred style for large houses was the Queen Anne, then very out-of-date architecturally. By 1912 and 1913, when Craftsman-style houses were being built by the dozens in Kitsilano, Grandview seemed to have slumped, and most of the construction then taking place was in symmetrical builders' styles on small lots.

At the southeast corner of Victoria Drive and Napier, there stands another of Grandview's great buildings—the W.H. Copp house. Built for a realtor whose business, Copp and Mutch Real Estate and Financial Brokers, was prospering in the Vancouver of 1909-1910,

21. The house at 1138 Lily Street.

the house was designed by the architect J.P. Malluson. Although it has been divided up into suites for decades, the house has lost little of its character and still retains its holly hedging, formal evergreen landscaping, and architectural detailing, including the extensive leaded glass and the bellcast turret with spire. Note the garage at the rear of the property, designed to match the house in a manner seen usually in the coachhouses and gatehouses of areas such as Shaughnessy Heights. It is interesting to speculate on the impact that such lavish residences had on the cautious, frugal city administration—the water permit for the house, signed by Copp himself, contains a pencilled notation "with permit for fountain," implying that if Copp was going to waste water on a decorative fountain, he would be charged for it.

Just to the north of Copp's house, on the block facing Victoria Drive and stretching from Napier to Parker, are two very large houses that are the legacy of a contractor named John C. Hawkins. The oldest house, at 1090 Victoria Drive, has been a private hospital since the First World War years, when it was known as the Grandview Heights Hospital. Hawkins completed it early in 1906, and it occupied the whole block for a few years until he built the house at 1020 Victoria Drive. It is difficult to trace Hawkins himself, and to get an idea about what he actually did: in some years during the period from 1905-1912, he is listed in directories as retired, and in others as a carpenter. Although he was definitely the owner of 1090 Victoria Drive, it is not clear whether he actually lived there, as the 1907 and 1908 directories list him as resident at the northeast corner of William and Salsbury. Regardless, he was a builder and, because of the hybrid nature of the houses he owned and/or built, was probably his own designer. Recently, 1090 Victoria Drive has been put through an extensive rebuilding program that has left little of its original fabric intact.

Whereas 1090 Victoria Drive was a typical Colonial Revival bungalow design, with a pleasantly rambling feel heightened by its bellcast eaves and dormers, the house at 1020 Victoria Drive, built in 1910, is a fascinating amalgam of late nineteenth-century architectural styles **(22)**. Its gambrel-roofed side dormers and round turret are traceable to Norman-style buildings such as those popularized in the 1880s in New York State by the famous architectural firm of McKim, Mead and White; although the architectural tradition on which these were

22. The house at 1020 Victoria Drive, built in 1910 by John Hawkins.

based is a sixteenth- and seventeenth-century French one, very similar elements appeared at almost the same time in the Richardsonian Romanesque style. Probably the best stylistic description of the Hawkins house at 1020 Victoria Drive is Shingle style, which, in the 1880s and early 1890s on the eastern seaboard of the United States, brought together all of the above-noted features and added to them a wrapped, patterned skin of wooden shingles and widely curving, bell-cast rooflines. The house has additional local decorative features such as the alternating smooth and rough-cast concrete blocks forming its base, and superb curved double-hung windows and leaded glass set into the turret. It is a *tour de force* of design and craftsmanship, exceeded only by the quality of the next house Hawkins built for himself—a more elaborate version of this hybrid style, erected in 1912-1913 at 1927 West 17th Avenue, in Shaughnessy, while Hawkins was still living at 1020 Victoria Drive.

Turn west (left) at Parker Street.

Although there are interesting houses all along Parker Street west of Victoria Drive, the most striking building is the large, Shingle-style house at 1829 Parker, erected in 1909 as an investment for lumber-company owner W.W. Stuart, who lived at 1825 Robson Street near Stanley Park and owned a mill on Front Street West (the south side of False Creek west of Main Street) **(23)**. It has an exact duplicate at 364 West 10th Avenue in Mount Pleasant. An interesting part of the design is the third-floor sleeping porch, framed by curved eaves and featuring a rounded shingle-covered entranceway. The researchers of the City of Vancouver heritage inventory speculate that 1829 Parker and 364 West 10th Avenue were built from a design in a house-pattern book. In the mid-1920s, you could have taken music lessons at 1829 Parker from Edith Blake, and been assured of your safety by the presence nearby of

23. The Stuart house at 1829 Parker.

T.H. Butler, the manager of the Merchants Police Patrol, who both lived at and worked from the house at 1872 Parker.

The contrasts in the development of Grandview are again sharply visible at the corner of Parker and Salsbury, a hundred yards away from Stuart's imposing house. The two little bungalows on the northwest corner were erected in 1909 by an unknown builder for the above-mentioned speculator J. Lennox Wilson. They are especially significant because they are the earliest known examples of houses with wraparound windows at the corner of the living room, a feature that is next seen in late-1920s California Bungalows, then in the stucco-sided 1930s starter houses built all over the Lower Mainland, and finally in the 1950s houses that are typical of residential neighbourhoods such as the University Endowment Lands **(24)**.

Even more of a contrast, although fitting in very well with modern Grandview, is Salsbury Court, the large apartment building erected in 1911 at the southeast corner of Salsbury and Parker **(25)**. A wood-framed structure with brick veneer, it was designed by Arthur Julius Bird who, a few years previously when he was City Architect, designed Fire Hall Number 6 on Nelson Street in the West End and, in

24. The speculator's cottage at the corner of Parker and Salsbury, with its wraparound livingroom window.

25. The 1911 Salsbury Court at the corner of Salsbury and Parker.

private practice, the Afton Hotel on East Hastings Street. About fifteen years later, Bird appears in directories as the city building inspector.

Turn south (left) on Salsbury Drive.

The grandest building on Salsbury Drive is "Kurrajong," directly to the south of Bird's apartment building. As described above, "Kurrajong" was completed in mid-1907 to the designs of an unknown architect for the Australian immigrant J.J. Miller **(26)**. To this day, it retains its period feeling, enhanced by the holly landscaping

26. "Kurrajong" about 1907. (Photographer unknown, CVA)

27. The "fence of all sorts" in the lane between Parker and Napier.

and massive retaining wall built of concrete blocks, which are also used for the foundation and base of the Queen Anne-style building. It has been a private hospital since the 1920s; in 1937 it received an interesting Streamline Moderne addition to the east, by the architects Townley and Matheson. Note a more recent addition to the property—the "fence of all sorts" in the lane, erected by the property manager from bits of wood over the past ten or so years **(27)**.

Across the street from "Kurrajong," and erected a year later, is one of the largest BCMT&T prefabs ever built—the Robertson Presbyterian Church, with vertical battens covering the joins between the prefabricated panels. The church was raised during a renovation that added metal windows and the wheelchair ramp in 1984.

A block to the south of this church, at the northeast corner of

28. Early Vancouver Specials on William Street.

William and Salsbury, are three very early Vancouver Specials **(28)**. Erected in the late 1950s, these houses feature the boxlike shape, extremely low-pitched roof covered in tar and gravel, unarticulated stucco facade, upstairs kitchen and living areas with a thin balcony to the front, and downstairs bedrooms typical of the much-maligned "Special"—a ubiquitous building style that is regrettably the closest Vancouver has ever come to producing an indigenous architecture. (The flat-roofed, post-and-beam, West Coast Contempo style popularized in the 1950s by architects such as Ron Thom and Arthur Erickson is an evolution of 1930s and 1940s International-style houses built in Los Angeles by architects such as Richard Neutra and Rudolph Schindler. Post-and-beam structure was the most popular method of building a California "rancher" in the immediate postwar period.)

Turn west (right) onto William and walk to Commercial Drive.

The tour finishes at Commercial Drive, where you can choose among a myriad of cappuccino bars and observe the ever-changing nature of "The Drive." Commercial development began along these blocks about 1907, corresponding to the growth of the residential neighbourhoods on adjoining streets. The B.C. Electric's interurban railway line linking downtown Vancouver with New Westminster and the Fraser Valley proceeded east along Venables to Commercial Drive, where it turned south and ran along the centre of the street until it reached Vanness and the

29. The well-preserved grocery store dating from 1907 at the corner of Venables and Commercial.

private right-of-way now occupied by the SkyTrain system.

A few stores and buildings on that part of The Drive still reflect the early days of the interurban railway and the settlement of the adjoining streets. The oldest store is the wooden building at 902–916 Commercial, erected in 1907 and with a water permit signed by A.F. Arnold—probably one Albert F. Arnold who worked for Canadian Financiers **(29)**. The Florida Market at 1102 Commercial was built the following year, and the B.C. Block at 1046 Commercial was finished in 1910 for a drygoods operator named John Campbell.

Like Strathcona, the Grandview area evolved without the strict controls considered necessary by contemporary planners and residents in areas such as the Municipality of Point Grey (see Chapter Seven). Although that fact is historically interesting, the significant question raised by an area such as this is whether this type of picturesque, almost-random type of neighbourhood could ever evolve again. The answer is: probably not.

It is instructive to compare Grandview with Kerrisdale. Although the latter had much more rigid planning in terms of lot layouts, setbacks and servicing, it had no design guidelines as such; instead, it developed in its more-or-less coherent way because there appear to have been many shared values among the people who settled there, with any excesses tempered by the general *lack* of prosperity. Even though, in theory, much bigger houses could have been built, they were not, partly because people did not have the money, and partly because a common aesthetic emphasized the modest house within its garden. Recent development in the Kerrisdales of the Lower Mainland has reflected an entirely different set of values: maximum house, minimum yard, maximum ostentation to the streetfront and privacy within and to the rear. As well, architectural styles have changed radically, and the tradition of craftsmanship which made older houses complementary regardless of their stylistic differences has vanished.

The wide differences seen in Grandview—the result of the divergent individual visions of what the neighbourhood would become—were not moderated or controlled by planning or zoning. Huge house sits next to cottage which sits next to apartment building. But it all hangs together, if only because all of the buildings were part of the same tradition of craftsmanship, regardless of their specific architectural style or dimensions. No such tradition influences the megahouses that have recently been inserted onto multi-lot property assemblies, such as the building at 57th and West Boulevard or a number of the edifices built on the Southlands flats near Balaclava Street. These houses do not respect the surrounding architecture or the informal landscape in which they sit, whereas a house like "Kurrajong" is a huge Queen Anne among more modest Queen Annes.

The example of Grandview, or of Strathcona, suggests that land should be "unzoned," with no absolute right to develop anything and with each application approved on its individual merits using a combination of design and neighbourhood criteria. This could not happen under current planning orthodoxy, as all owners within a certain zone are considered to have equal rights to square footage and type of development. Land ownership and development equal money and business, according to the current system, regardless of generalized public concerns about aesthetic quality or social usefulness or neighbourhood impact—or, usually, heritage preservation.

It will be impossible to change this until there arises a public consensus that ownership of land confers no rights without corresponding responsibilities—that is, that property development carries with it some obligation of neighbourhood awareness. But, in an area where there are large numbers of individual owners, who would decide what type and how much development was appropriate? What guidelines could be developed and administered? It is only in comprehensive developments, where a single owner controls an area and has the desire to build a village or a town, that this type of diversity could be planned. In theory at least, a gentle chaos could be programmed, as is the intent with neo-traditional town schemes such as Bamberton on Vancouver Island.

Regardless, if we cannot develop this type of neighbourhood again in areas of multiple ownership because our traditions or our standards have changed, it becomes crucial to preserve the neighbourhoods that still exist. Although land development in areas without strict planning controls was obviously motivated mainly by the desire to make money, that is also the motivation in today's highly controlled urban environment, with the result only that our neighbourhoods are becoming ever more homogenized.

Delamont Park

¹/₂ HOUR

eritage buildings often manage to avoid demolition because of circumstances that have nothing to do with a desire on anyone's part to preserve anything at all. One highly visible example of that truism is the row of old houses on Pacific Street, just to the west of the downtown end of the Burrard Bridge, which were finally restored in the early 1980s. Although they had been in what was originally a desirable location, a mere block from the waterfront, they lost much of that advantage once the bridge opened in the early 1930s and traffic increased to tremendous volumes on Burrard and Pacific streets. Having thus been rendered unattractive, they missed the great redevelopment boom which—caring not a titch for heritage—scythed through the West End in the 1950s and 1960s. By the early

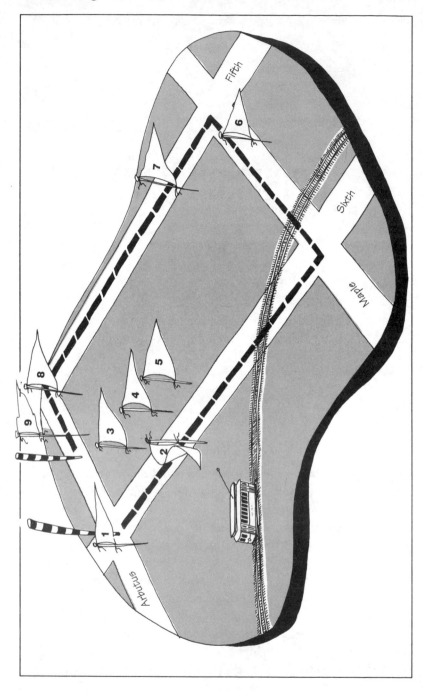

1980s, they were one of only a few surviving rows of old houses left in the area.

A similar set of "non-heritage" circumstances has preserved, so far, some very early houses in the eastern part of Kitsilano, on two blocks bounded by Arbutus, 5th Avenue, Maple, the railway tracks, and 7th Avenue. Now surrounded by apartment buildings, these houses were purchased beginning more than thirty years ago by the city, which was assembling land for a planned freeway-type roadway dubbed the Burrard-Arbutus Connector. As commuter traffic heading towards Mackenzie Heights and Kerrisdale tended to bottleneck at the dogleg between Burrard and Arbutus, a connector, following the line of the old B.C. Electric interurban tracks from 6th and Burrard to Broadway and Arbutus, was envisioned to ease the flow.

These houses were purchased before they had a chance to be bought up and demolished by apartment developers, but the connector idea, like the rest of the freeway schemes of the 1960s and early 1970s, foundered on the shoals of the anti-freeway public sentiment expressed in the civic election of 1972. Casting about for a use for the land so laboriously assembled, the city then decided the area was short of open space and designated the land as a future park site. A small area along the railway tracks between 7th and 6th avenues was actually developed with little swings, berms, benches and evergreens; it was named Delamont Park after Arthur Delamont, the long-time leader of the Kitsilano Boys Band. There was, however, no political will to uproot the rest of the tenants and bulldoze the houses in the midst of Vancouver's chronic rental-housing shortage.

Even though the houses are in varying states of repair, and range in historic value from the important to the insignificant, they are in sum one of the great heritage enclaves in the city—especially the block of 6th Avenue east of Arbutus. And, because most of them are city-owned, they present an opportunity equalled only by Nelson Park (Chapter Three) for restoration as part of an innovative heritage park. As is the case in Nelson Park, the future of these houses is in some doubt, due to hard times for the city's tax base and some difficulty getting the city and its parks board together to come up with a solution.

The first European activity in the area, after Jerry Rogers's loggers went through it in the 1860s and 1870s, was the construction in 1891 of an orphanage, Alexandra House, on 6th Avenue in the block east of what is now Burrard Street (it burned down in the mid-1970s). At the time Alexandra House was built, Vancouver was home to fewer than ten thousand people, most of whom lived in wooden houses on narrow lots throughout the downtown and Strathcona areas, and in more elaborate houses in the West End; the only significant congregation of people south of False Creek was in Mount Pleasant, near the road to New Westminster (now Main Street and Kingsway). The next area to be subdivided and opened up to settlement was the Fairview Slopes in the early 1890s; it and Mount Pleasant received streetcar service in 1891 on a belt line that crossed the Granville Street and Main Street bridges. The proximity of streetcars travelling on Centre Street north of 9th Avenue (Granville Street north of Broadway) and the expansion of sawmilling activities on the south side of False Creek encouraged people to settle in what was then known as West Fairview, and has been called Kitsilano since 1905.

In the vicinity of today's Delamont Park, the first recorded settler was a man named George V. Orimus, a "tooldresser" (according to the city directory) who probably toiled for one of the False Creek sawmills an easy walk away; he bought property at the southwest corner of 6th and Maple, built a house, and in March, 1899, had it connected to the city's water system, which at that time was being extended west from the Fairview Slopes area. Meanwhile, both the B.C. Electric Railway Company, which operated the city's streetcar system, and the Canadian Pacific Railway were considering extending transportation systems through the sparsely settled district. As early as 1891, the Canadian Pacific Railway had seen the potential of a rail connection between its main line at Burrard Inlet and the distant fishing village of Steveston and the farms of Lulu Island. In 1891, the CPR incorporated the Vancouver and Lulu Island Railway, with superintendent Harry Abbott as president; however, it did nothing about surveying a line until 1900. By that time, the CPR had abandoned its plans of establishing a deep-sea port at Kitsilano Point, and so began to encourage the BCER to build a streetcar line along the English Bay waterfront.

The V&LIR dispatched its first passenger train from downtown Vancouver to Steveston on June 30, 1902. Instantly dubbed the Sockeye Limited, the train made only two stops in what is now suburban Vancouver: at Magee Road (49th Avenue, the nearest point to the long-established Southlands farms of the McCleerys, Hugh Magee and Henry Mole) and Eburne (the sawmilling site near the south end of Granville Street). The rail line crossed False Creek on the Kitsilano trestle, just west of today's Granville Island, ascended the slope on a wide double curve, and headed southward along the line of today's Arbutus Street. Three years later, the CPR leased the tracks to the BCER, which electrified them and commenced a regular interurban service that survived until 1952. (The lease has since reverted to CP Rail, which operates it as a short line to service the few remaining industrial customers in that part of Vancouver; the right-of-way is coveted by everyone from the CPR property development department to rapid-transit planners to advocates of a bicycle route to downtown.) The description from the *Province* of a ride on the line on opening day, July 4, 1905, makes much of the fertility of Lulu Island fields and farms but says little about the Vancouver part of the journey: "After crossing False Creek, the line climbs the heights of Fairview around what is known as the Horseshoe, so named from the double curve which the line takes to get up the grade. Heavy forest with occasional farms is passed until Eburne is reached. . . ." The two Kitsilano-area stations on the Vancouver-Eburne interurban were at Broadway and "Millside"—4th and Fir. In 1908, the line was double-tracked, and that year's timetable shows that Steveston was thirty-seven minutes away from the Broadway station.

The *Province* reporter actually passed several of the houses which still exist on the Delamont Park blocks. The oldest surviving house is the one at 2020 West 5th Avenue, dating to May, 1900, and not in terrific condition today. Much more significant, however, is the cluster of houses built the following year on Arbutus Street and 6th Avenue.

Start at Arbutus and 6th Avenue and walk east, circumambulating the block counterclockwise.

The block's landmark is the Arbutus Grocery at the southeast corner of 6th and Arbutus. With its false front, drop siding and corner entry, it is one of the finest old grocery stores in the city **(1)**. False-fronted commercial buildings got their start in the boom towns that

1. The Arbutus Grocery, at the corner of 6th and Arbutus.

sprung up during the California gold rush in 1849, the idea being to make a simple-to-build gabled or shed-roofed building appear more urban and important, like the masonry buildings of established towns and cities. The Arbutus Grocery itself dates from 1907 and was built by Thomas F. Frazer, who had lived on the block since 1901, when he built a house next door at 2084 West 6th. Probably Frazer's original house on the site was little more than a cottage, which he replaced some years later (perhaps about 1920) with the California Bungalow that now graces the site. When Frazer built the grocery store, he put on his water-permit application that he would be using water for a cow or horse: he quite possibly had both—one to give milk and the other to pull a delivery wagon through the neighbourhood.

The surviving 1901 houses on the block include J.R. Murphy's house at 2078 West 6th. It was hooked up to the water system on the same date as Frazer's original house next door, raising the possibility that one of the men built both of them (although the similarities between Murphy's house and the two Roland Scarlett houses on Arbutus, described below, suggest that Scarlett might have built them all). The other 1901 houses are the C.F. Jones house across the street at 2085 and the southernmost one of the two Roland Scarlett houses

2. The 1901 Murphy house at 2078 West 6th Avenue.

on Arbutus. The Murphy house is the most unusual architecturally. Probably best described as a builder's version of the Shingle style, it is an open, airy house with a cross-gabled roof, a deep front porch and a prominent front dormer growing out of the main roof pitch, which is set off-centre on the house's front facade **(2)**. The front door is at the side and set well back from the front wall and bay window of the living room, creating an L-shaped front porch. Rambling and rather ungainly builders' houses like this were quite common in the West End and the residential parts of downtown Vancouver until the 1950s and 1960s. The Jones house across the street is a more common design—a simple gabled builder's house with Queen Anne flourishes, especially the fishscale shingles (sometimes called feathers) in the gable and the off-centre wraparound front porch **(3)**.

The next house built on the block was a 1906 one that used to stand on the little piece of Delamont Park just to the east of 2068 West 6th, which was built in 1907 by J.R. Murphy as a next-door neighbour to his 1901 house. Murphy's 1907 house is a variation on typical builders' Vancouver Boxes of the time. Its distinguishing feature is a large dormer, gussied up with turned wooden columns, that grows out of the main gable—a feature of Murphy's 1901 house next

3. The 1901 Jones house at 2085 West 6th Avenue.

door and of the Scarlett houses. Across the street, the C.J. Church house at 2075-7 was built in 1909 and is yet another builders' house type; its semi-hipped roof in the front gable forms a facade like much English cottage architecture **(4)**.

4. The 1909 Church house at 2075-7 West 6th Avenue.

5. *The Brodrick bungalow at 2055 West 6th, with the house at 2059 to the left.*

The house at 2059 dates from 1913; with its fancy Carpenter Gothic fretwork in the gable, it is a throwback to the Victorian-era houses of neighbourhoods like Strathcona. Although built three years earlier, the F. Brodrick house at 2055 was a very modern design for the time: it is an early California Bungalow, the kind of single-storey house that began to appear about 1905 in American architectural pattern books extolling the "Pasadena Style" **(5)**. Its neighbour next door to the east was a 1906 house, since vanished; the site is now occupied by a small daycare centre. Completing the streetscape is the

6. (left) *The four 1912 houses at the southeast corner of 5th and Maple, built by the Vernon brothers' contracting firm.*
7. (right) *The Brownlee house at 2020 West 5th, built in 1900 and the oldest house on the block.*

Vancouver Box at 2027, built in 1909 by B.H.L. Thersteinsson, which has been boarded up for a number of years.

The vacant lot next door holds an allotment garden established by the locals. It, and the "City Farmer" demonstration garden at the northeast corner of 6th and Maple, are the overlay onto this Edwardian-era neighbourhood of early-1970s Kitsilano karma.

The four houses on the east side of Maple Street between 6th and 5th, just to the north of the "City Farmer" building, were completed in 1912 by the Vernon brothers—John, William, Lewis and Norman —who operated a contracting business **(6)**. All are variations on the Craftsman style, and none is owned by the city. Rounding the corner onto 5th Avenue, and passing by the blank apartment building, you arrive at 2020 West 5th. Built in 1900 for a labourer named Thomas Brownlee, it has been greatly altered with stucco and cheap aluminum windows **(7)**. Like Brownlee's house, the rest of the houses lining 5th Avenue on the gentle slope up to Arbutus Street are all city-owned, and present a golden opportunity for restoration as a period streetscape. Although no one of these houses is anything special as they now stand, restored they would be an asset to the city. Numbers 2032 and 2038 were speculatively built by a carpenter named Roy Cowan in 1910;

8. The 1905 Queen Anne-style Boyd house at 2090 West 5th.

2044, 2050, and 2058 were built respectively in 1907, 1911 and 1905; the Vernon brothers built 2062 and 2068 in 1910; 2078 and 2086 were built in 1905 and 1910; and the little stucco box at 2088 occupies the site of another early house, one built in 1900 for a marine engineer named E.C. Turner.

The different dates of construction of these houses on the same block demonstrate one of the great heritage truisms of cities like Vancouver—that historic streetscapes were in their early years a combination of houses and vacant lots. It is only very rarely that a block was built up all at once; the Macdonald Street houses between 5th and 7th avenues are one such example. If the city should decide to do a "heritage park" incorporating some of these houses, the unrestorable or badly deteriorated ones could in theory be removed, leaving "vacant lots" scattered among them as little finger-parks.

The grandest house on the block occupies the corner at 2090 West 5th Avenue. Built in 1905 for a lumberman named J.F. Boyd, it is an elaborate, expressionistic version of the Queen Anne style **(8)**. The two main gables on the roof form an L, and the curving, bellcast rooflines are matched by the inward-curving profiles of the eaves at

9. *The 1907 house built by Roland Scarlett at 2128 Arbutus, on the northern third of his city lot; the corner of his 1901 house is visible on the right of the photograph.*

the bottom of the gables. This type of gable treatment appeared only occasionally on Vancouver houses—"Wilga" in Grandview originally had the same treatment.

Just to the south of the Boyd house, the three remaining buildings on the block are the legacy of a cabinetmaker and carpenter named Roland Scarlett, who built the centre one at 2134 Arbutus for himself in 1901. It is quite similar in its rambling character to the Murphy house of the same year at 2078 West 6th—an off-centre, jumbled mixture of rooflines and dormers. The L-shaped oriel window in the upper gable is very unusual. Even more odd is the fact that it is a full-sized house built sideways on a fifty-foot-wide lot, the same year as C.F. Jones was building his more conventional house at 2085 West 6th.

Having purchased his one single-family lot, 50 feet wide by 120 feet deep, Scarlett decided to add a second house to it, at 2128 Arbutus, in 1907 **(9)**. This house, with its front dormer incorporated into the peaked roof, is very similar to the two Murphy houses on West 6th Avenue. Three years later, not being content with two buildings on a single lot, Scarlett added the unusual bay-windowed apartment building with a parapet like a little wooden castle on the remaining thirty-foot by fifty-foot vacant piece, creating a very dense little enclave with a floor-space-ratio at least equal to that of the large apartment buildings elsewhere in Kitsilano. Evidently, there was little control on builders in pre-World War One Kitsilano. The City of Vancouver now owns the apartment building, but the two earlier Scarlett houses are owner-occupied private dwellings.

In addition to all of these houses, and the arcane history of which they are a record, take a few minutes to consider the equally interesting views. The streetscape east of Arbutus on 6th Avenue, taking in the gravel swales on the edge of the paved roadway and some stone walls and old buildings, is an authentic piece of old Vancouver. Much of Kitsilano looked like this in the 1950s and early 1960s, and now only these blocks survive. The view from 7th Avenue, looking north along the railway tracks to the Thersteinsson house, with glimpses of the city in the distance, is also worth contemplation.

Kitsilano

1 1/2 – 2 HOURS

The blocks of Kitsilano on either side of Macdonald Street north of Broadway are a well-preserved area of modest, middle-class housing from the years between 1910 and 1925. Although the blocks farther to the east were subdivided earlier, comparatively few interesting houses survive there due to widespread apartment redevelopment during the past thirty years. Not surprisingly, the middle-class nature of Kitsilano becomes less apparent close to the beach, where a number of luxurious estates were established shortly after the beginning of this century. Evidence of many of these still exists today.

The significant boundary in Kitsilano is Trafalgar Street, originally called Boundary Road, as it is the dividing line between the Canadian Pacific Railway Company's land grant to the east and

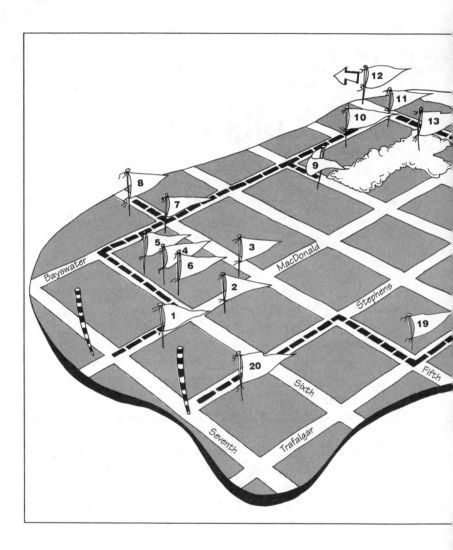

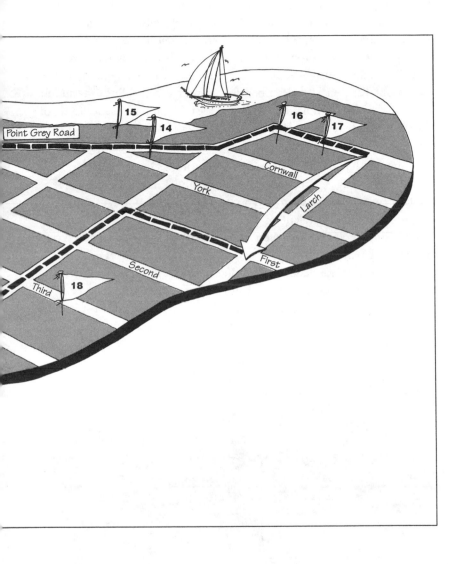

District Lots 192 and 540 to the west, which were owned by private individuals. In 1885, the CPR had received a land grant from the province of about six thousand acres, including much of Vancouver's downtown area and land south of False Creek between Trafalgar and Ontario streets, as a reward for extending its rail line to the Granville Townsite (today's Gastown). On the part of this land grant in today's Kitsilano, the most historic and consistent area still extant is the Delamont Park enclave described in Chapter Five; at the easternmost end of the CPR lands, on the blocks of Mount Pleasant south of Broadway and west of Ontario Street, another historic enclave of houses from the turn of the century also survived, and has been restored.

The first half of this walk meanders through District Lot 192, bordered by Trafalgar, Broadway, Balaclava, and English Bay; this piece of land was first surveyed in August, 1860, and purchased for the pounds-sterling equivalent of $388 by Colonel R.C. Moody of the Royal Engineers. To the west it adjoined a Government Reserve, vestiges of which still remain in the old seaplane base near Jericho Beach and the army base and housing west of Alma Street above 4th Avenue. Subdivision of the original government reserve created District Lot 540, which, in the Kitsilano neighbourhood, is the land between Balaclava and Alma streets; it was subdivided in 1909-1910

House building near 4th and Waterloo, about 1910, with the contractor's wagon stuck in the mud. (Photo by James L. Quiney, CVA 7-20)

by R.D. Rorison and sold by J.L Quiney, to whom reference is made below. In the years just before the First World War, some of the finest Craftsman-style houses in the city were built in this area, especially on Dunbar and Collingwood streets north of 4th Avenue.

The name "Kitsilano" dates from 1905, when the CPR began to promote the land bounded by Cedar Street (now Burrard), 4th Avenue, Trafalgar and English Bay. The company asked Jonathan Miller to come up with a suitable name. Miller, who had arrived on Burrard Inlet in the early 1860s, served as constable of the Town of Granville and later as Vancouver's first postmaster, and had become very wealthy through canny purchases of real estate throughout the city. He consulted with local residents and received advice from the well-known local anthropologist Charles Hill-Tout before settling on the name Kitsilano, after the legendary Chief Khahtsalano of the local Squamish band. At that time, Khahtsalano's grandson August Jack still lived at the village of Snauq on Kitsilano Point—now the site of the Planetarium, museums and archives.

Start at the corner of 7th Avenue and Macdonald.

For a suburban real-estate development to be successful, transportation to the city is essential. In recent decades, that has meant the provision of a road system out to the nearest arterial or freeway, but in 1908 it meant a streetcar or interurban service. Accordingly, the owners in District Lots 192 and 540 lobbied the B.C. Electric Railway Company for a streetcar line on 4th Avenue, which was laid and went into service on October 23, 1909 (streetcar service on 9th Avenue did not commence until 1911, the year when that street's name officially became Broadway). The 4th Avenue streetcars ran from Granville and Smithe across the newly completed Granville Bridge—which had opened for traffic a few months previously and which reached the south side of False Creek at 4th Avenue—then proceeded west along 4th to Alma Road. Development of the blocks around 4th and Macdonald commenced then.

The long row of—at first glance—identical rooflines stretching down the east side of Macdonald Street between 7th and 5th avenues is evocative of old Vancouver to many people. However, this sort of

1. Two of the Vancouver Boxes built in 1912 by the carpenter Joseph Nixon on the east side of Macdonald Street between 6th and 7th avenues.

consistency of building type was rare in the city during that period; usually, a builder erected at most two or three houses, and by the time the adjoining lots were developed another builder or owner was involved, with a somewhat different idea of style or responding to a different market or economic climate.

The four houses occupying the southern end of the block between 6th and 7th are examples of the Edwardian Builder or Vancouver Box style, and were completed early in 1912 by the carpenter Joseph Nixon **(1)**. They are symmetrical, upright, rather formal houses, with the eaves surrounding the gable forming a well-defined triangle and a neat little pediment above a stoop at the front door. Variations on this style were built by the thousands all over the Lower Mainland (and all over North America, in fact) in the first decade of this century. By the time of their construction, the style of these houses was already out of date; its replacement was a more woodsy, picturesque idiom known as the Craftsman style.

The twelve houses occupying the narrow lots north of Nixon's little enclave were originally identical or mirror images, and were

2. The 1911 Craftsman houses by the carpenters Lockie and Miller on the east side of Macdonald, looking north from 6th Avenue.

built by the contractor/carpenters Lockie and Miller in 1911 **(2)**. No one of these houses is particularly special, although they all demonstrate to varying degrees the hallmarks of the Craftsman style: decorative brackets along the eaves, wooden posts on full-width porches, exposed rafter ends, and shingle siding (in some cases now covered with asbestos siding or stucco).

Compare the Lockie and Miller houses with the two Craftsman-style houses, built at the same time, at the southwest and northeast corners of 5th Avenue and Macdonald **(3)**. They are both in the Craftsman style, but are a variation usually called the Swiss Cottage or Swiss Chalet, because they have side gables, and a fore-and-aft roof pitch inspired by the vernacular architecture of rural Switzerland. Other elements of the Craftsman style visible in these houses are the sleeping porches off the main bedroom, a common feature on houses of that time due to the penchant for sleeping in the open air; the leaded-glass windows or lead-lights illuminating staircases and forming a transom above the three-part windows; and the rough clinker bricks set at odd angles into the mass of the chimney.

Most of the Lockie and Miller houses, and the four Joseph Nixon houses to the south of them, illustrate the classic fate of old Vancouver houses—they have been modernized and altered, some of their porches filled in, some wooden windows replaced by cheap aluminum sliders, and some extra doorways cut to effect the houses'

3. The 1912 Swiss Cottage at 2103 Macdonald.

transition from single-family use into the self-contained suites so typical of Kitsilano. Few houses in Kitsilano are stylistically pure and also in original condition; the best-preserved of the Lockie and Miller houses is the one at 2216, south of 6th Avenue, but even its cedar-shingle roof has long since been replaced by an asphalt-shingle one, and it has lost its shed roof over the second-storey front window.

Although the houses facing onto Macdonald are not necessarily in very good condition, it is unlikely that any of them will be torn down in the foreseeable future, because they are very large on their very small lots and no new structure could be built to that scale under the existing zoning by-laws. Many of the houses are rented to tenants who occupy small housekeeping rooms and suites or flats; the afford-ability of these apartments contributes greatly to the social character of Kitsilano, but it also provides little economic incentive for the owners to restore or even to maintain their buildings. In the future, then, it is likely that these houses will be restored during a conversion into self-owned flats, or possibly will be "deconverted" back to their original use as single-family houses.

This process of gentrification—seen elsewhere in Mount Pleasant and Strathcona and in old neighbourhoods throughout the towns and cities of British Columbia—has actually reduced the population of Kitsilano from about thirty-six thousand twenty years ago to about thirty-two thousand today. The block which concludes this tour—Stephens Street between 6th and 7th—contains a number of houses that were rooming houses twenty years ago but have now been reconverted into quite grand, single-family heritage houses.

Large houses of the late Victorian era, when times were prosperous and there was an emphasis on formal, almost ritualized standards of dress and behaviour, were designed with a myriad of special-purpose rooms, such as libraries and ornate parlours. It is ironic to see fashions come full circle in the 1980s and 1990s, when new houses are once again being built with a myriad of special-purpose rooms, now called media rooms and offices and children's wings. In their room layouts, the Edwardian-era Kitsilano houses are quite different from the late-Victorian houses in that they have a casual, open plan, strongly influenced by trends from southern California; the California Bungalows seen later on this tour, although not built until the 1920s, were designs that had been developed in Los Angeles before the First World War.

Turn west (left) on 6th Avenue.

The block of 6th Avenue west of Macdonald Street is an excellent example of how city streets developed in the early years of the century. On the north side, there is a row of tall, finely crafted pre-World War One houses, abruptly ending about midway down the block; across the street from them is a school, General Gordon, whose construction just before the First World War was prompted by the rapid population growth in the area, and which was named after a recent English military hero. To the east of the school, on the south side of the street, are some low bungalows, built just after the First World War. To fill in the rest of the block, there is a smattering of houses from later generations, including a 1920s Tudor hybrid at 2869, a stucco starter house from the late 1930s at 2875, an early-1980s townhouse on the site of a corner store at the northeast corner of 6th and Bayswater, and a mid-1980s duplex with large front-entry garage at 2861-2863. This mixture of housing styles is typical of neighbourhoods all over Vancouver because of the roller-coaster economy—several houses are built, the economy crashes, then several years later it booms again and a couple more houses get built in a different style.

The first house on the block was 2841 West 6th, completed in

4. 2837 and 2841 West 6th Avenue, the earlier pair of houses by the Pettigrew brothers.

1911 a few months before its neighbour at 2837; both were built by the carpenters Thomas and William Pettigrew **(4)**. Evidently, the Pettigrews had bought four lots, and used the sale of 2837 and 2841 to finance the construction of 2851, where they subsequently lived, and 2855 West 6th, which they sold **(5)**. The two early houses show Queen Anne influences, with their narrow eaves, tall windows, off-centre bay windows on the second floor, and oval door glass; the two later houses are much more vertical and symmetrical, and have Craftsman-influenced heavy wooden brackets and deep eaves to give them a sense of structure and shelter. The Pettigrews' spec-built house at 2855 West 6th is the most interesting because it is such a hodge-podge of styles, being a bit of Craftsman and Vancouver Box mixed in with ornate Ionic columns holding up the front porch. No one could have accused the Pettigrews of having pure tastes!

Note the technological differences between the Queen Anne and the Craftsman styles. Queen Annes, such as those seen in the Nelson Park and Strathcona areas, share with other nineteenth-century housing styles tall windows, narrow eaves and bay windows—all for the purpose of allowing the maximum possible amount of light into

5. *2851 and 2855 West 6th Avenue, built by the Pettigrews in 1912.*

the house. The Craftsman style, by comparison, has very heavy over-hanging eaves and deep porches, for they were really a southern California house designed for bright light and a hot climate. However, the Craftsman houses adapted well to the Pacific Northwest and the west coast of Canada because of the availability of electric light, which compensated for the darkness of deep porches and broad eaves. The interiors of nineteenth-century Queen Annes are usually chopped up into little rooms, most with fireplaces, capable of being separated from each other by parlour doors or pocket doors for the purpose of con-serving heat; Craftsman houses, as adapted to regions north and east of Los Angeles, were able to maintain open plans due to the availability and affordability of central heating, especially the hot-air furnace.

The other old houses on this block that are stylistically interesting are the two hipped-roof, Arts and Crafts buildings erected in the summer of 1913 by the builder John J. Keenlyside at 2825 and 2831 West 6th, just to the east of the first Pettigrew houses **(6)**.

As this area has become more desirable in recent years, there has been a notable change in the old, neighbourly streetscapes. New resi-dents arrive with the expectation that they can accommodate their cars off the streets, even if it means parking them in the front yards in

*6. 2831 West 6th Avenue, one of the two houses erected in 1913
by the contractor John Keenlyside.*

blocks such as this one where there are no back lanes. At 2851 West
6th, the old house has been restored, but the front yard has been
paved for a parking space—a very unsympathetic form of landscaping
for Vancouver. The recently built duplex at 2861-2863 takes this one
step further by paving the entire front yard and digging it out to provide ramp access to two double garages; the house and its front deck
are thus separated and insulated from the street. If the heritage character and neighbourliness of Kitsilano's streets is to survive, new residents are going to have to adapt to the neighbourhood, rather than
expecting the neighbourhood to adapt to them.

Turn north (right) at Bayswater and walk to 5th Avenue.

The house at the southeast corner of Bayswater and 5th, with a
street address of 2926 West 5th, was built in 1911 for William Warner
(7). This is a good example of a builder's Queen Anne. Most Queen
Annes in Vancouver were modest wooden houses like this, notable
mainly for the asymmetrical profile created by the turret set into one
corner. This type of house was once very common in the West End,
and is now seen most often in the Grandview-Woodlands area. It was

a style that had run its course by about 1905, but scattered examples such as this one were built right up into the First World War period.

To the west of Bayswater, on both sides of 5th Avenue but most consistently on the south side, is the epitome of a subdivision in the Garden City of the early 1920s **(8)**. These simple, low houses with low-pitched roofs, solid porch posts, broad front porches and an open-plan living area are called Pasadena Bungalows or California Bungalows, a style that evolved in the rapidly growing suburbs of Los Angeles beginning about 1905. Migrants flocked to the Los Angeles area for its so-called "Pasadena lifestyle" which was, in a design sense, an outgrowth of the Arts and Crafts movement, but in a practical way reflected the desire of many people for a simple life in an affordable house set within a manageable garden. The ground-level basements on these 5th Avenue houses are not representative of the original style, which was lower to the ground as southern California houses had no need for a furnace and extensive coal and sawdust storage.

7. (left) *The 1911 Queen Anne-style Warner house at 2926 West 5th Avenue.*
8. (right) *The California Bungalow at 2974 West 5th Avenue.*

All of the bungalows on West 5th Avenue adhere to the Craftsman ideal of a mixture of surfaces, including the clinker brick in porch posts and chimneys and the creative use of wood in shingle patterns and brackets and carved bargeboards. They all look the same at first glance, but many have individual touches, such as the Japanese-inspired pointed peak and rounded brackets on 2970 West 5th, built in 1919 by the carpenter Fred Melton (the rounded brackets and bargeboards were part of what in California was some-times referred to as an "Airplane Bungalow," two good examples of which in Vancouver are the houses at 6592 Maple Street and 6795 West Boulevard in Kerrisdale).

The bungalows on the south side of the street were erected by two groups of builders between 1919 and 1921. The five houses immediately to the west of the corner of Bayswater, numbered 2950 through 2978, were built in 1919 and 1920 by Fred Melton (1879-1956), a Cornish contractor who had arrived in Vancouver in 1906. His later efforts in the Kitsilano area include the brick Lilfred Lodge (named presumably after his wife, Lillian, and himself) at Balsam and Cornwall, and Melton Court at 2310 Cornwall, where he spent the last years of his life.

Farther west on the block, the firm of Cook and Hawkins began construction around the beginning of 1921 on the group of six California bungalows at numbers 2990 through 3030. Like Melton, W.J. Hawkins and C. Cook were carpenters, the latter living at 2210 Balaclava Street.

Compared with the large houses on relatively small lots that were a feature of the early blocks of this tour, these California Bungalows do not have anywhere near the same amount of floor space per lot area (known as FSR—floor space ratio—the measure of a building's density on its lot). As current zoning and building by-laws allow a higher FSR on the lots than that of the bungalows, there is considerable incentive to demolish them. Preserving this type of housing is becoming difficult for a number of reasons. First, lot values have ascended into the stratosphere due to the zoning and desirability of the area; second, the bungalows cannot be added to without wrecking their character, as witness number 2996, drastically altered in the late 1970s by an iconoclastic owner; and third, current city policy deters addition of backyard buildings in order to develop the lots to their maximum development potential.

Continue north on Bayswater towards the beach.

The example of the house at 2890 West 3rd shows what is most likely to happen under current by-laws. There was a bungalow on the site that could not be added to; neither could another dwelling be built behind it on the lot, so the old house was demolished and a new

9. *The new triplex at 2890 West 3rd Avenue (under construction), designed to fit into the historic streetscape.*

triplex has been erected in its place **(9)**. The fact that the new triplex, designed by Stuart Howard Architects, is very neighbourly and a sympathetic addition to the streetscape does not change the fact that a heritage house—part of the original historic streetscape—was removed and replaced by a new-old building.

The large, turreted wooden duplex at the southeast corner of 3rd and Bayswater was designed by Spaceworks Architects in the early 1980s. It is a front-yard infill for the 1909 cottage, built for Chester S. Rollston, that still stands at the back of the lot. The cottage is one of the last examples in Kitsilano of the semi-rural character that was soon replaced by the more regimented blocks of builders' houses through which you have just passed. The loss of its tidy, front-yard orchard is regrettable; however, the redevelopment of the property was done with great sensitivity, and was probably the first—and possibly the last—redevelopment project in Kitsilano that did not commence with the clearing of the lot.

Just to the north along Bayswater Street is one of the most interesting enclaves in the entire city: Tatlow Court, a Tudor version of the Los Angeles bungalow courts that were very popular there around 1920 **(10)**. In southern California, bungalow courts were built in every style from Spanish Colonial to Hansel and Gretel, sometimes consisting of very small detached cottages, other times of sets of semidetached buildings; the buildings or cottages were always small and quite intimate, and they shared a common courtyard and an entrance through some sort of formal gateway.

Tatlow Court, designed in 1927 by the architect Richard Perry and completed the following spring for developer H. Rosenblat (the president of a Chrysler dealership called Fordyce Motors at 1291 Granville Street), is a casual mixture of Arts and Crafts influences, especially notable in the lovely lychgate forming the entrance to the court, and a late-1920s romantic Tudor or Period style. The central court is almost overgrown with shrubs and trees, making it difficult for a passerby to see very far into the private inner space. The buildings are four side-by-side duplexes, two on the north side of the court and two on the south, and a fourplex at the east (rear) end. In the

10. Tatlow Court, at 1820 Bayswater Street, in 1933. (L. Frank photo, VPL 5299)

space at the northeast corner of the property there is an allotment garden for the residents; at the southeast corner there is a small parking lot. The actual density of the project is about twenty-four units per acre—double that of single-family houses on thirty-three-foot lots—yet there is little evidence of large numbers of buildings or any sort of density or crowding. Tatlow Court survived a demolition threat in the 1970s, and was subsequently renovated to add sympathetically designed second storeys to the units.

This type of design is not only interesting historically but could serve as an inspiration for new developments offering a combination of privacy with shared occupancy and maintenance of the substantial piece of open space in the central courtyard. For families with small children, it offers the prospect of shared supervision and a neighbourly, communal enclave. Its major drawback, at least in terms of typical development norms, is that the units have to be quite small, both to retain a good balance between open space and built space and to put enough families into the court to make it work as a little community. Tatlow Court seems to achieve this balance very well, and certainly—by comparison with townhouse and small apartment projects

that do not house many more people per acre—creates an atmosphere closer to the ideal of a cottage in a village that many people seek unsuccessfully when they consider the purchase of a single-family home.

(There are a few other courts or mews developments within a couple of blocks of Tatlow Court, on 4th Avenue between Bayswater and Balaclava. Developed by the Central Mortgage and Housing Corporation after the Second World War, these mews houses are built at a higher density than Tatlow Court—about thirty units per acre—and although less luxurious and picturesque than the older example, they are affordable little rental communities with many of the advantages noted above.)

Immediately adjoining Tatlow Court's northern boundary is a stone wall surrounding a substantial 1950s apartment building. The wall dates to 1908, and the completion by John and Jessie Hall of a very fine home called "Killarney," which old photographs show to have had granite foundations and a Craftsman-style roofline and detailing **(11)**. It originally stood on two-and-one-half acres, with nearly two hundred feet of frontage on Point Grey Road and six hundred feet of grounds running back along Bayswater to 3rd Avenue. Accounts mention its superb leaded-glass windows and the sprung ballroom floor in the basement. In the years before Jessie Hall's

11. *"Killarney," about 1915.* (Photographer unknown, CVA Bu.P.113)

death in 1949, "Killarney" was the centre of Kitsilano society, as well as of Conservative politics and the operations of the local chapter of the Victorian Order of Nurses.

John Hall was the city's first notary public, and had parlayed his early arrival in Vancouver (in 1885) and real-estate and business skills into a considerable fortune. Jessie Hall was even more of a pioneer, having been born in the Cariboo in 1872; she was the daugher of Sam Greer, who after years of mining and homesteading in the interior moved to the coast, where he claimed in 1882 to have purchased or pre-empted land along what became Kitsilano Beach. Greer and family settled along the beach, far away from the tiny settlement of Granville (Gastown), two years before the Canadian Pacific Railway determined that Burrard Inlet was to be the railway's terminus and subsequently received the grant from the provincial government of six thousand acres of the future city, including the Kitsilano area. With its eye on a future deep-sea port for Kitsilano Point (see below), the CPR promptly began legal proceedings to evict Greer from his little piece of arcadia; the legal skirmishing, climaxing in an eviction order signed by Judge Matthew Baillie Begbie, was followed by a brief gun-fight, the wounding of Sherriff Armstrong, the capture of Greer, and his conviction in September, 1891, on a charge of common assault. As so often happened in Canadian history, the CPR got its way, but Greer could take some comfort in the fact that Greer's Beach remained for about twenty years the popular name for Kitsilano Beach. Eventually a street, running for all of a block from Cypress to Chestnut just north of Cornwall, was named for him. He died in 1925 at the age of eighty-two.

Following Jessie Hall's death, the house was sold and eventually demolished in February, 1956, prompting numerous nostalgic news-paper articles noting the "passing of an era," but reflecting the general feeling that nothing could stand in the way of progress. It was, after all, the 1950s. There was no awareness then anywhere in North America that old mansions could become luxurious flats, or that new buildings could be added to the grounds of historic ones. The apartment building that replaced "Killarney" retained the name of the old house, and has an imposing yet gracious facade and large, high-ceilinged rooms inside. Built by Whitsell Construction, it was a progressive

X-shaped edifice with fifty-six units, each one an outside suite, that "left more garden and landscape than any other big building in the city." Although not supported by the Technical Planning Board because it exceeded the recommended density for the area, city council approved it and rezoned the site in September, 1955.

The Halls' arrival in 1908 had marked the end of a period when this part of Kitsilano was far out in the country, past the outward spread of the city. Prior to about 1908, Kitsilano (or West Fairview, as it was sometimes called) was centred farther to the east, with most houses and shops within walking distance of the False Creek sawmills, the Fairview Belt Line streetcar and, after 1905, the Kitsilano streetcar running from the beach to downtown across the Kitsilano trestle. By 1907, the expanding population in the area justified the erection of the West Fairview School on 4th Avenue between Yew and Vine (until very recently the site of Plimley Motors), which in the final years before its demolition in 1946 was the Seaview School for the training of Royal Canadian Air Force cadets. The brief tour of the Delamont Park area (Chapter Five) explores a surviving couple of blocks from that era.

Far to the west of the Halls, the lone occupant of what was known as District Lot 540 was the family of James Quiney, who settled in the forest at the northeast corner of Dunbar and 4th Avenue in 1907 on land purchased from R.D. Rorison. Before buying that property, the family had tented at the foot of Alma, drawing their drinking water at the foot of Dunbar Street from a solitary tap placed on the city water line extending to the Jericho Golf Course some distance to the west. For a time, the family had a bear cub as a pet, and the children carried the family groceries home from downtown through the salmonberry and salal thickets along the old Indian trail that became Point Grey Road. After a couple of years of such homesteading, Quiney became a real-estate agent and began selling lots on the newly cleared streets near his wilderness home.

In 1909, the Quineys moved to a new house they had built at 1820 Waterloo, still standing today, and decided to get rid of the bear. After a brief and unsuccessful stint as mascot for HMCS *Rainbow* (the Canadian navy's antiquated protector of the Pacific Coast following the Royal Navy's withdrawal from Esquimalt in 1910), the bear found a new home in Stanley Park; in a letter dated August 16, 1911, the Quineys were advised that the Board of Park Commissioners wished to "express...their thanks and appreciation of [their] kind donation of a brown bear to the Stanley Park zoo."

Apart from homesteaders like the Quineys, there were summer campers—usually West End residents—who tented along Greer's Beach and the seashore farther to the west. According to old stories, husbands used to row out from Vancouver to spend Sundays with their holidaying families. The earliest campers along the Kitsilano seashore were probably the Crickmay family, who spent several summers in the late 1880s and early 1890s in wooden-sided, canvas-roofed huts near the foot of Bayswater Street. William Crickmay's major business venture was the erection of the Imperial Opera House on the north side of Pender Street at Beatty; opened in 1889, it had a two-year pre-eminence in the city until the CPR's opera house opened at Granville and Robson. Some years later, the Imperial was converted into a roller-skating rink; the roller-skating business later moved to a landmark campanile-towered building on the triangle bounded by Denman, Morton and Beach on English Bay. In 1889, William's son Alfred founded one of the early customs brokerages in the city—Crickmay and Bermingham—which operated in the city for a half-century.

Sharing the beach at the foot of Bayswater with the Crickmays and other campers during the 1890s was the English Bay Cannery, one of a myriad of small operations processing the bounty hauled from Burrard Inlet. It was purchased in 1905 by the businessman and soldier Robert Douglas Rorison, who was the major landowner in the nearby District Lot 540. A year later, it caught fire, leaving as a legacy on the beach a gleaming pile of snipped tin and solder. Rorison dismantled the damaged cannery buildings, used part of the timber to repair cottages on the shore and, using the best structural timber, built a large, turreted Queen Anne house a couple of blocks to the west at 3148 Point Grey Road **(12)**. Many years later, in the 1960s, his home on Point Grey Road achieved some notoriety as the "Peace House," before being sold. During its reconversion into a single-family house, it was stripped of its fine detailing and old-fashioned windows, then rebuilt with spare vertical siding and picture windows. The Queen Anne design is an anomaly amid the cottages and Craftsmans of that part of Kitsilano.

12. The Rorison house at 3148 Point Grey Road, about 1912.
(James L. Quiney photo, CVA 7-88)

Walk eastward (towards downtown) along Point Grey Road.

The park to the east of "Killarney" is named for Robert Garnet Tatlow, who was a member of the city's first park board in 1888 and served continuously until 1905 **(13)**. More significantly, he was a prominent Conservative politician and businessman until his accidental death in 1910, caused when the horse pulling his carriage through the Victoria streets bolted and pitched him onto the pavement. In addition to his real-estate and insurance interests, Tatlow had made a considerable fortune in the fish-packing business with H.O. Bell-Irving, and rose to prominence provincially as the minister of finance in the government of Sir Richard McBride during the first decade of this century. Tatlow Park remains today one of the truly tranquil spots in the city, with little Tatlow Creek meandering through a meadow dotted with weeping willows.

13. Tatlow Park, looking north about 1915 with "Seagate Manor" in the distance.
(Photographer unknown, CVA)

Across the street from Tatlow Park is an open sward created quite recently by the demolition of some fine houses. The idea of clearing all the buildings from the north side of Point Grey Road to give motorists an unfettered view of English Bay and the North Shore mountains dates back to the late 1920s, and the city plan drafted by the American planner Harland Bartholomew. The same plan advocated the construction of the Burrard Bridge and the upgrading of Cornwall Avenue and Point Grey Road as fast routes linking the Point Grey suburbs and UBC with the downtown. Although periodically revived by civic politicians since the 1950s, the idea of public ownership of the bluff above the bay has never received very wide city support, if only because of the enormous cost of acquiring such prime real estate.

Regardless, the occasional piece of property has been purchased and promptly converted into a landscaped vacant lot—these little parks, like teeth knocked out of a smile, are visible every half block or so between the foot of Macdonald and the foot of Trafalgar, and in a few spots to the west as well. The problem with these bare, windswept parklets, other than their cost per square foot, is that they allow more noise, heretofore buffered by the houses along Point Grey Road, to get through to the foreshore below, which is in something of a natural state and is a pleasant contrast with the groomed and raked sand of Kitsilano Beach a few blocks to the east.

The most important house removed to create parkland was "Seagate Manor," designed by Thomas Hooper in 1912, which stood on the eastern end of the open space at the foot of Macdonald until its demolition in 1977. Built for lumber-company owner Thomas Jenkins, it was sold in the 1920s to grain-elevator operator E.A. Woodward, then later was converted into suites which were, in the 1970s, occupied by about fourteen senior citizens. The considerable support within the community for the retention of the house and its affordable housing, with a park fashioned out of the existing garden, did not prevent its demolition.

A block to the east of the site of "Seagate Manor," the Ells house stands on the high side of the road, a landmark in the neighbourhood since 1908 **(14)**. With its symmetrical hipped roof, dormers and wide verandah, it is a good example of the Colonial Revival style, and for years had a beautiful garden, with large camellias planted almost against the house. A development proposal in the early months of 1992 sought to move the house slightly to the west and restore it, demolish another house to the east, and build a townhouse complex on the land remaining. The Ells house is historically interesting at least in part because it appears to have been built for a grocery clerk, William Ward Ells, who worked for the H.A. Edgett Company, known as "The Store of Plenty," at 153 West Hastings Street. Either

14. The 1908 Ells house, on Point Grey Road at Stephens Street.

15. *"Edgewood," on Point Grey Road just to the east of the bottom of Stephens Street, as it appeared in the early 1940s, shortly before its demolition.*
(Dominion Photo Company, VPL 26502)

Ells had a source of capital apart from his job or else he speculated successfully on real estate, as did many other Vancouverites in the boom years before the First World War.

The Ells house was erected four years after and across the street from the first house built in that part of Kitsilano. "Edgewood" was a magnificent home, designed by architect Capt. W.H. Archer, with its grounds occupying the entire block above the beach from the CPR boundary at Trafalgar Street to Stephens **(15)**. According to city archivist J.S. Matthews, it was in its day considered to be "The Finest Home West of Granville Street." Its owner was a pioneering real-estate salesman named Theodore Hatton Calland, who bought the land about 1902 and tented with his family along the beach for a couple of summers before building his mansion. In their first years there, Calland and family lived an interesting existence that was a combination of homesteader and squire: Calland often hired horses to show remote Fairview property to his clients; before the Kitsilano streetcar commenced operations to Kitsilano Beach in 1905, he rode his bicycle along the rutted roadways to Granville Street to catch a tram for downtown; on other days, he rowed a skiff to work; once, when his wife became ill, she had to be carried by stretcher through the bush to the streetcar terminus at Vine Street. Yet "Edgewood" was home to elegant garden parties, such as the one in 1907 where a lady named Mrs. Bulwer bemoaned the duplication of many street names to the west of "Edgewood," and suggested that those streets be renamed for English battles. It was agreed, and Alderman Calland arranged that Boundary Road should become Trafalgar; Richards, Balaclava; Cornwall, Blenheim; Lansdowne, Waterloo; and Campbell, Alma. "Edgewood" was demolished in the early 1940s, shortly before Calland's death, and the land subdivided.

As noted at the beginning of this walk, Trafalgar Street is the significant boundary in this part of Kitsilano, separating the Canadian Pacific Railway lands to the east from the privately held lands to the west. On the slopes just above the beach, the best remaining illustration of the freewheeling nature of early development west of the boundary is the brick Wellington Apartments at Trafalgar and 1st; also, it is worth noting that the Callands and the Halls bought entire blocks of land on which they established estates or, in the Halls' case with land they owned south of "Killarney," subdivided and sold as small lots. Compare that with the houses on the east side of Trafalgar, all built on *lots* purchased from the CPR, which had graded them and provided basic services.

The first house built on the CPR lands along Cornwall Avenue is the Roy MacGowan house at 2575 Cornwall. It is a fine example of the Colonial Revival style and, like "Edgewood," was built in 1904— before the area was named Kitsilano and before streetcar service commenced into the area. The three MacGowan brothers— Alexander, Max and Roy—ran a successful shipping and insurance business under their own name.

Walk north (towards the beach) on Trafalgar, then east on Point Grey Road.

A slightly later house, built on three lots and still retaining its expansive grounds, is the W.H. Forrest house at 2590 Point Grey Road at the bottom of Trafalgar Street **(16)**. It is one of the best examples locally of the Shingle-style buildings first erected in the 1880s in such eastern seaboard states as Massachusetts and Rhode Island. Fittingly, a later occupant of this seaside house was John Andrew Cates, a member of the family whose towboat operations are

16. The Shingle-style house built in 1908 for W.H. Forrest at the foot of Trafalgar Street.

still a feature of the North Vancouver waterfront. Several Cateses have had political careers both municipally and provincially.

The foot of Trafalgar Street, being the western boundary of the CPR lands in Vancouver, was also the end of the track for the transcontinental railway. In the late 1880s, while considering alternatives to the Burrard Inlet waterfront for its railyards and deep-sea port (the former were constricted by the steep bluff along the edge of what is now downtown Vancouver and the latter compromised by the strong tides through First Narrows), the CPR ran a rail line across False Creek on a small trestle and along the English Bay waterfront to the foot of Trafalgar, where a stop block marked the end of track. Although rumours abounded for a few years that the CPR wished to build its port at Point Grey, and plans were actually developed and published for a dock, industrial and hotel complex on Kitsilano Point, the company allowed itself to be bribed by the city with offers of tax reduction and free water and established its railyards on the north side of False Creek (the Expo site), keeping its passenger operations and ocean port on Burrard Inlet. At some point around the turn of the century, the tracks to the east of Trafalgar were torn back to about Vine Street. The bank cut forming the pathway above the beach between Balsam and Trafalgar is the old railway roadbed. The tracks to Kitsilano beach and the access to downtown Vancouver across the

17. The Craftsman-style Logan house at 2530 Point Grey Road.

Kitsilano trestle were taken over by the B.C. Electric Railway Company in the summer of 1905 for a streetcar line which stayed in operation until after the Second World War. In the 1960s, city archivist Major J.S. Matthews proposed a design for a small commemorative cairn at the foot of Trafalgar, but nothing came of it.

Another early building in this exclusive area is the fine Craftsman-style house at 2530 Point Grey Road, which was designed by Honcyman and Curtis in 1909 and erected for Matthew Sergius "Sea Wall" Logan (1866–1952) **(17)**. Born in Morrisburg, Ontario, Logan first arrived in New Westminster with his family in 1875, but they soon returned to Ontario; Logan himself came to settle in 1899 and went into the lumber business. As a parks commissioner from 1916–1919, he was a strong advocate of a Stanley Park seawall, something that was not completed until years after his death. The house was later occupied by General Victor Odlum (1880–1971), the son of Edward Odlum of Grandview and a noted soldier, Prohibition advocate, newspaper publisher and politician. Although modified from its original state—much of the fine woodwork, including the sunburst motif in the main gable, which was originally half-timbered, is not original—the house itself has always been treated sympathetically and remains an excellent example of the Craftsman style. Note the two houses on either side built as infills on what were the original expansive grounds; both were built in the 1970s and are of such fine quality that they complement the old house, even though the one to the west is in a French Second Empire style that is quite foreign to Vancouver's architectural tradition.

Walk south (up the hill) on Larch Street to 1st Avenue.

After carefully crossing the exceptionally busy Cornwall Avenue (named, along with York Avenue immediately to its south, for the Duke and Duchess of Cornwall and York, later King George V and Queen Mary, who visited Vancouver in 1901), and recollecting that Cornwall was a tranquil residential street until the Burrard Bridge opened in the early 1930s, you ascend the hill into the Kitsilano apartment district. The transition of this area from single-family houses began in the mid 1950s with a decision to allow conversions of old houses to suites (which had been going on for years anyway) and new apartment construction. The process was relatively uncontroversial until the early 1970s, when developers began erecting highrises on the slope; following vociferous protests in early 1974 about the tower known as "Carriage House" at 3rd and Balsam, and a proposal to build a highrise on Cornwall, the city bowed to public pressure and banned any further tall buildings. Redevelopment has nonetheless continued, and most of the old houses have been demolished and replaced by townhouses and small apartment buildings, many of which have been quite successful as designs and have reinforced the neighbourly streets of the blocks above the beach.

One of the old houses that was converted into suites and had a new building erected on its grounds is the Stearman house at the southwest corner of 1st Avenue and Larch. Built in 1908, the year before the 4th Avenue streetcar line opened the area to general settlement, the elegant house has a monkey-puzzle tree to match its period look, although it is now difficult to see through the filigree of shrubbery. The way that the tower was incorporated into the curving roofline was typical of eastern American Shingle-style houses of the 1880s. It was built by an unknown architect for William Charles Stearman (1873-1960), a pioneer hardware merchant whose experiences during the Klondike gold rush prompted him to wear a nail as a tie pin. "Anyone can buy a pearl sticker, but show me a man who can find a common nail," he explained. He was a master of picturesque advertising, employing slogans such as "Get 1-2 day 4 Xmas gifts 4-2-morrow may B-2 late!"; the sign on his Granville Street hardware store featured a neon cow, the letter "4," and his name, which afficionados knew to mean "Steer For Stearman's." His name survives today in the Stearman lock company.

Walk west on 1st Avenue, then turn south (left) on Trafalgar Street.

The Stearman house is one of the last of the grand houses on the hill above the beach. Twenty years ago, there were other fine homes on the south side of the block west of Stearman's, but they were demolished in the 1970s and replaced by the condominiums seen there now.

On a more modest scale, the blocks of 2nd Avenue and 3rd Avenue, on both sides of Trafalgar, have retained most of the old houses from the period just before the First World War. Notable early houses are the Mills house at 2590 West 2nd Avenue, a very fine example of Craftsman design, and the turreted 1911 Queen Anne at 2556 West 3rd Avenue **(18)**.

Trafalgar Street between 4th and 5th avenues again shows the differences in development on opposite sides of the CPR boundary. On the eastern, railway-owned side, there are some fine houses, most notably the two 1911 houses built by the carpenter John McLeod at 2054 and

18. The 1911 Queen Anne at 2556 West 3rd Avenue.

19. The Panama Apartments at 5th and Stephens.

2060 Trafalgar, the latter of which has an elegant semicircular porch. By contrast, there are apartments on the other side of the street, dating from the same period: at the northwest corner of 5th and Trafalgar, the three-storey building was called the Panama Apartments in the 1920s; the row of apartments behind it was known as the Panama Annex **(19)**. Both were built in 1911 by a contractor named George W. Robertson, who lived a half-block away at 2651 West 6th Avenue.

On its main floor, on the corner side, the Panama Apartments had as a tenant the Rourke Brothers grocery store; it was one of a half-dozen small groceries within a six-block radius that, like many of the groceries of Strathcona, have disappeared. The independently run local groceries have lost popularity beside the more aggressive 7-11 and Mac's Milk chains, and have lost their distinctiveness because of the extended opening hours now maintained by big supermarkets like Safeway. It being Kitsilano, however, there are independently run organic produce outlets, such as the one at the corner of 4th and Trafalgar, providing for a specialty market; the oldest of the organic markets, the Naam, on 4th just west of Stephens, got out of the produce business years ago, and has adapted to the changing times by buying a cappuccino machine.

Walk west on 5th Avenue, then south on Stephens Street.

Much of 5th Avenue between Trafalgar and Stephens streets was built up before the First World War. Unlike the large, pre-World War One houses that stood on Macdonald Street (at the beginning of the tour), many of the 5th Avenue houses here were quite small, almost like cottages, and jeopardized by ever-increasing land costs. An example of the kind of redevelopment attracted to this part of Kitsilano by small houses on expensive lots is the front-back duplex at 2646–2648 West 5th Avenue. Originally, a cute, storey-and-a-half cottage barely big enough for a small family occupied the narrow lot, but as it could not be added to, it was demolished. Although the new duplex presents a complementary and well-designed facade to the street, it extends a considerable distance into the backyard—far past the point to which the other houses on the block extend. Compare this with the tall triplex at 2890 West 3rd, viewed earlier on this tour—if small buildings must be replaced, this is another potential solution.

The tour concludes on the block of Stephens Street between 6th and 7th avenues, which, with the neighbouring blocks of 6th Avenue and Macdonald Street form one of the most consistent heritage enclaves in the city. The oldest house on the street is 2232 Stephens, completed late in 1911 by Island Investments, a company controlled by a building superintendent named Daniel C. Kay, who lived not far away at 3118 West 1st Avenue and had his offices downtown in the Rogers Building **(20)**. Operating under that same company name, Kay completed the two houses to the south, at 2238 and 2242, early in 1912. The remaining five houses on that side of the block were built by another of his companies, Canada West Developments, in the spring of 1912. All of the houses are variations on the Craftsman style; most are "Swiss Cottages." All eight houses on the west side of the block, numbers 2203 to 2245, were built in the summer of 1912 by the contractors Bentley and Wear, who had their office at 2042 Granville Street; they are all Swiss Cottage Craftsmans.

Although twenty years ago most of these houses were divided up into rooms and suites, they have since been reconverted into single-family homes or else have been expensively modified into condo-

20. The east side of Stephens Street between 6th and 7th avenues—
2232 Stephens, the oldest house on the block, is the one farthest to the right.

miniums. Because of this trend, there has been a loss of population in the area and arguably a change in the character as the neighbourhood has gentrified. The neighbourhood has in fact come full circle, back to the well-maintained single-family style it had when it was new eighty years ago. Although this evolution is sometimes bemoaned because it represents the loss of affordable housing and "funky" character, the real problem in the Lower Mainland, and in cities elsewhere, is that we are not building any more Kitsilanos: houses with the ability to metamorphose and evolve as they age.

Kerrisdale and Third Shaughnessy

2 HOURS

I n the years just before the First World War, the Kerrisdale area was touted as Vancouver's "sunny southern slope—the place for your permanent home," with easy access to the city by the B.C. Electric Railway's interurban system. Even though two miles of bush and swamp separated Kerrisdale from the city limits at 16th Avenue, piped water arrived in 1912 from the City of Vancouver's Capilano reservoir, the Municipality of Point Grey laid sewers, and electricity and telephone could be procured by those who wished—thus, the necessities for suburban development were available to prospective buyers and home builders.

The interurban railway connecting Steveston and Marpole with Vancouver and passing through the Kerrisdale area was the major

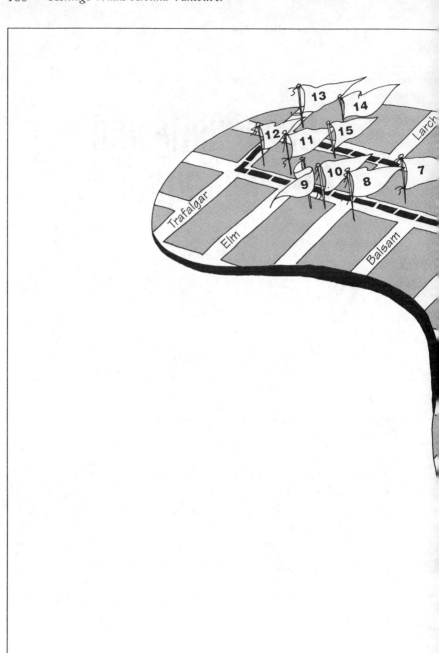

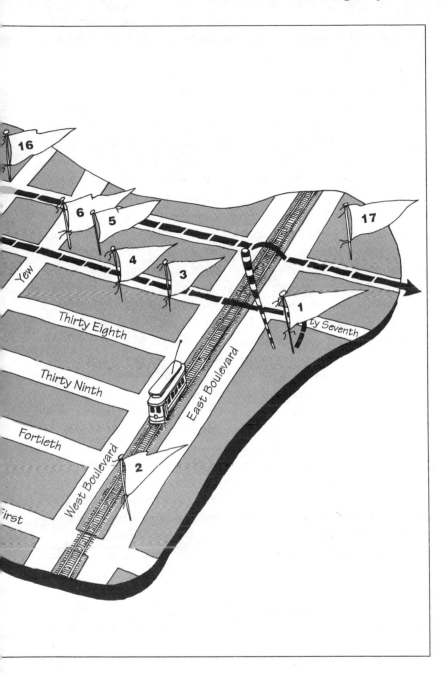

spur to the area's development. Prior to the commencement of the
B.C. Electric's service in the summer of 1905, there were only a few
houses on large properties dispersed among the stumps and mud of
the district. The electric interurban railway superseded a Canadian
Pacific Railway branch line that had operated on the same tracks for a
few years; another legacy of the CPR's activities was a large cleared
field at the northeast corner of Wilson Road (41st Avenue) and the
railway tracks, which was used to grow produce for the company's
hotel and railway operations. Now known as Kerrisdale Field at its
southern end and the site of Point Grey School on its northern end,
the field was originally called the CPR Gardens.

Local politics made the Kerrisdale crossroads a significant centre of
the Vancouver suburbs. Vancouver's civic boundary was 16th
Avenue, and the miles of logged-over scrub and scattered houses
between there and the Fraser River constituted a separate, single community—the Municipality of South Vancouver, incorporated since
1891, with a municipal hall on Fraser Street near 41st. The residents
west of Main Street felt that their community's great expectations
were being jeopardized by the unwillingness of South Vancouver's
politicians and the voters on the east side of the muncipality to
borrow and tax adequately for such capital improvements as roads,
sewers, schools and beautification, including street trees. Although the
western residents had one of their own, the Councillor E. Foreman,
as reeve of South Vancouver in 1906, they were unable to obtain the
desired reforms, and so seceded in 1908 and incorporated the
Municipality of Point Grey. Its headquarters were established at
Kerrisdale, in a Tudor-style municipal hall at 42nd and West
Boulevard, the site now of the Kerrisdale Community Centre. Both
Point Grey and South Vancouver joined the City of Vancouver in
1929, creating the city boundaries still in existence today.

The sales pitch by local real-estate agents brought to the Kerrisdale
area a type of citizen who, by and large, wanted a substantial and
attractive but not ostentatious home. In the years from 1912 until the
1930s, the streetscapes gradually filled with attractive and gracious
houses; the area soon had a settled and well-tended look, with lush
landscaping and marvellous street trees, that survived with little dis-
ruption until the house-building and paving frenzy of the late 1980s.

Regardless, it is possible to see within a few blocks on either side of the old railway line all of the typical middle-class housing styles built in the city in the decades before the Second World War.

The Third Shaughnessy area, into which you venture for the last half of the tour, is a grander community, the result of the land development policies of the Canadian Pacific Railway in the prosperous mid-1920s. Its name results from the fact that it was the third subdivision of the CPR's vast Shaughnessy tract of land stretching southwards from 16th Avenue between Arbutus and Oak streets. First Shaughnessy (originally known as Shaughnessy Heights), between 16th and 25th, was developed before the First World War, and is the city's grand showplace from the pretentious Edwardian era. After the First World War, the CPR developed Second Shaughnessy, the blocks between 25th and 37th avenues, in a much more modest style. Third Shaughnessy, bounded by 37th, Maple, 41st and Granville, was advertised for sale to the public in February, 1926, and ten years later was almost completely built up. The large block of land bordered by 33rd, 41st, Granville and Oak streets—directly to the east of Third Shaughnessy—was mainly occupied by the Shaughnessy Golf Club, opened in 1912, closed in the early 1960s. A portion of the old golf course is now the home of Van Dusen Botanical Gardens; residential blocks and Eric Hamber School occupy the balance. In addition, between 37th and 41st, there are blocks of housing dating from the 1920s and 1930s, clustered around the Gothic Revival-style Vancouver College, designed in 1924 by the architects Twizell and Twizell. One piece, bounded by 37th, 41st, Osler and Hudson, was put on the market in March, 1928, as Selkirk Heights.

Recently, these distinctions have been muddied, as the historical uniqueness of Vancouver's community names increasingly falls victim to the sloppiness that afflicts so much of contemporary language. Both Second and Third Shaughnessy are sometimes called South Shaughnessy, a name also applied, often by eager real-estate agents, to the very different Kerrisdale area south of 41st Avenue. The cachet of the Shaughnessy name has even caused it to be extended to the north and west of First Shaughnessy, effectively burying the old name of Talton Place for the blocks of 13th through 16th avenues west of Burrard Street under the new name "Lower Shaughnessy."

Reflecting the prosperity of the late 1920s, which approached that of the period between 1908 and 1914, Third Shaughnessy has more of the expansiveness and graciousness of First Shaughnessy—some large lots and picturesque building sites on the curving streets, and many superbly landscaped properties. By comparison, the first few blocks of Kerrisdale through which the walk passes are decidedly modest and ordinary.

A walk through Kerrisdale and Third Shaughnessy is an excellent opportunity to examine the residential efforts of some of the noted architectural firms in Vancouver's history, and to compare them with the houses erected by the very talented builders who used a combination of stock house plans and their own experience and ingenuity to ply their trade.

Start at the corner of 37th Avenue and East Boulevard.

Designed in 1928-29 by the architectural firm Townley and Matheson, Point Grey School was commissioned by the Municipality of Point Grey shortly before its amalgamation with the City of Vancouver **(1)**. The school building is an excellent example of the Gothic Revival style, and is one of the early instances in the city of a poured-in-place reinforced concrete facade. There is a particularly fine auditorium occupying much of the middle of the original building, with a galleria of windows on two floors overlooking it. These windows have regrettably been covered up in recent years.

1. Point Grey School about 1930. (Photographer unknown, CVA Sch.P.1)

Fred Laughton Townley (the son of T.O. Townley, Vancouver mayor in 1901) and Robert Michael Matheson formed their partnership in 1919. The Capitol Theatre on Granville Street downtown was one of their first projects. The firm was also responsible for Tudor Manor on Beach Avenue, the Stock Exchange Building, several houses noted later in this tour, and—most significantly—Vancouver City Hall.

Note the house at 2057 West 37th Avenue, across the street from the school, which is easily identifiable behind its tall laurel hedge because its brick chimney is visible at what appears to be the front of the lot. This was part of the superintendent's cottage for the CPR Gardens, and sat originally on the site of Point Grey School. In the late 1920s, the cottage was moved across the street and inserted sideways onto the lot at 2057 West 37th, explaining why the chimney faces the street.

During the half-century before the interurban railway system ceased operation in 1952, passengers could board an electric train at a little wooden shelter a few yards south of 37th Avenue and be downtown in less than fifteen minutes **(2)**. The only drawback to this Lulu Island-Vancouver interurban line was that its terminus was some distance from the centre of downtown, originally on the northwest side of Granville Bridge, forcing passengers to walk downtown or to transfer onto city streetcars. Quite a grand station had been opened

2. *The interurban station a few blocks to the south of the 37th Avenue one, at 41st Avenue, in the summer of 1952, shortly before the Marpole-Vancouver interurban branch ceased operation. The view is across 41st Avenue from the southeast corner of East Boulevard and 41st.* (H.E. Addington photo, CVA Dist.P.104)

there in 1914, but eight years later, when traffic moved from the left-hand side of the road to the right, passengers were forced to cross railway tracks and increasingly busy traffic lanes to pick up a down-town streetcar; the interurban station was then moved to a remod-elled false-front store at the southeast corner of Davie and Seymour, where it remained until 1952 when the interurban system ceased to operate (the Marpole-Steveston portion of the line continued to run until 1958). A further extension into the heart of downtown, whether on the surface or underground, would have been a simple matter then, but Vancouverites soon became enamoured of anything that ran on rubber tires, and have since been unable or unwilling to re-create the simple efficiency and environmental compatibility of their turn-of-the-century interurban system. Such is progress.

Proceed west along 37th Avenue to Trafalgar Street.

The first two blocks of Kerrisdale west of the tracks are typical of most old areas of the city of Vancouver, in that there is little design consistency from house to house. Until a few years ago, these blocks had a few houses from the years before the First World War, a handful from the 1920s, and the balance from the 1930s through 1950s. The two-storey houses at 2160 and 2232 West 37th are the most notable pre-World War One houses here. They are good examples of the Craftsman style seen all over town.

As a general rule, Vancouver houses were at their tallest and most vertical in the late nineteenth century. Houses before 1914 remained tall, at least a storey and a half, although in the Craftsman style which became popular just before the First World War, the houses gave the impression of being lower because their broad roofs tied them more closely to the ground (see the "Swiss Cottages" later in this walk). The California Bungalow (several examples of which are described below) is a simple variation of the Craftsman style. It is worth men-tioning that the word bungalow, as used in the period from about 1910 to 1930, meant any comparatively small, simple house—it was not limited to low-slung, single-storey houses with verandahs like the originals in India, which were subsequently adapted throughout the British Empire.

Houses of the 1920s through 1950s in this area were often single-storey bungalows, initially the elegant California Bungalows of the period just after the First World War, but by the 1930s a myriad of stucco-sided starter houses (2130 and 2148 West 37th, for example) **(3)** and Spanish Colonial Revival boxes were popping up on vacant lots on every street. Part of this was fashion, but part was undoubtedly economics—buyers received less house for their money after the First World War.

3. (left) A 1930s "starter house," with octagon window, at 2130 West 37th.
4. (right) A classic Vancouver Special at 2166 West 37th.

The next wave of building in this neighbourhood in the years following the 1950s was the Vancouver Special, an excellent example of which is the house at 2166 West 37th Avenue **(4)**. The 1970s saw a return to more vertical and angular houses—thin, "mineshaft moderne," cedar-covered houses, such as those at 2178 2196 and 2332–2384 West 37th. Most of these have fitted quite well into the neighbourhood as they have been extensively landscaped with perennial, low-maintenance gardens; now, fifteen or so years later, some of the houses are almost engulfed by their shrubberies, an appropriate and pleasing fate for a lot of examples of architecture. More recent additions to the neighbourhood, most dating from the late 1980s, are the developer-built "monster houses," such as the ones at 2163 and 2175 West 37th **(5)** and at several locations along the 36th Avenue portion of the walk; typically, these houses feature a mix of Palladian windows and fanlights above the entranceway, a mixture of stucco and (often) fake brick or brick veneer on the facade, and very poorly

5. A late-1980s "monster house" at 2175 West 37th.

detailed and articulated aluminum windows that, because they lack adequate framing or are not recessed into their walls, always look like eyes without lashes in the middle of a blank, staring face.

Built respectively in 1922 and 1921, the houses at 2185 and 2195 West 37th Avenue are examples of the California or Pasadena Bungalow, and are the sorts of houses featured in "bungalow books" that were published in the years around the First World War by architects, many of whom were based in Los Angeles. Simple shapes, low-pitched roofs, and a mixture of woodsy and rough surfaces are typical of the style. The house at 2195 West 37th, which was the long-time home of Ernest Lackey, the manager of the Kerrisdale Theatre, has a picturesque look to it, largely due to the asymmetry of its porch and the heavy granite balustrade and foundations **(6)**.

A man by the name of Thomas Glover had the large Craftsman house at 2351 West 37th built in 1914. The little shack next door to the west was apparently built as a summer guest cottage.

At the crest of the gentle hill on 37th Avenue at Balsam Street, there is an enclave of old houses around St. Mary's Church that was inspired by a romantic sense of the picturesque and the Arts and Crafts style popular in late-nineteenth-century England. (The best example locally of this philosophy of building is the "little Cornish town" of Caulfeild on the West Vancouver waterfront.) On the 2300

6. *The 1921 California Bungalow at 2195 West 37th.*

through 2600 blocks of West 37th and West 36th, there is a consistent character—an amalgam of street trees, landscaping, fences and buildings, and the lack of curbs—that has managed to survive the stylistic fickleness of generations of owners, renovators and predatory builders.

The two finest houses are those at 2403 and 2427 West 37th, both designed by the architect George L. Thornton Sharp in 1912, the former for Prof. F.E. Buck of UBC (a prominent advocate of the City Beautiful movement), the latter for himself. The Buck house is a small, shingle-covered Craftsman **(7)**. Sharp's complementary home is in the Arts and Crafts style, strongly influenced by English medieval and rural architecture; compared with the imposing Tudor Revival houses that are such a feature of the Third Shaughnessy area, Sharp's is more like a cottage, with a simple, hipped roof line, although it has the half-timbering typical of both styles (it is very difficult to see due to the high hedge and trees in front). With their lush gardens and the supporting cast of nearby houses and St. Mary's Church, these two houses represent the best of the suburban Point Grey municipality remaining from the period around the First World War.

As a partner in the firm of Sharp and Thompson, George Thornton Sharp had a major influence on the city. The firm created the master plan for the University of British Columbia: a massive, grand assemblage of Gothic-style quadrangles, conceived in the heady

7. The Buck house, designed in 1912 by G.L. Thornton Sharp, at 2403 West 37th. The chimney pot of Sharp's own house is visible through the shrubbery on the left of the photo.

prosperity of pre-World War One Vancouver. The war, a sluggish economy, and the parsimony of the Liberal government of John "Dirt Farmer" Oliver, scotched the scheme, so that today only the library and the old science building, completed in the mid-1920s, bear witness to the original vision.

Sharp and Thompson's other well-known efforts in the city include the Vancouver Club on West Hastings, the pylons for the Burrard Bridge, and the Cenotaph at Victory Square. The firm eventually metamorphosed into Thompson, Berwick and Pratt, whose landmark buildings since the 1950s, most notably perhaps the B.C. Hydro Building on Burrard Street, transformed the city skyline.

Sharp and Thompson also designed the original Vancouver Art Gallery, which stood at 1145 West Georgia Street until the mid-1980s. The major patron of the art gallery was the businessman, watercolourist and amateur architect Henry Stone, whose sympathies with the Arts and Crafts style are evident in his house at Caulfeild (4648 Piccadilly Road South) and in his design of the charming St. Francis-in-the-Wood church there. In the years before 1918, Harry Stone lived in the house at the northwest corner of 49th and Larch (designed in 1912 by R. Mackay Fripp) and was a prominent member of the St. Mary's congregation—in 1913, he and his wife donated to the church the brass altar vases and hanging light fixtures in the nave and sanctuary. (Sharp donated the marble baptismal font; according to one source, the large hanging fixtures came from the CPR station at the foot of Granville Street, demolished about 1915.) Although most of Sharp's work in the 1910s and 1920s showed his fluency in traditional English styles, he designed the new art gallery in an austerely classical Moderne mode (the gallery was modified and expanded by Ross Lort around 1950 into the International-style edifice familiar to more recent generations of Vancouverites).

The centrepiece of the neighbourhood is the magnificent St. Mary's Church at the southeast corner of 37th and Larch, designed by Sharp and Thompson in 1913. It is the finest Arts and Crafts-style church in the city, with a superb wood-beamed interior, leaded-glass windows, entranceway and tower, all correctly aligned on an east-west axis. The congregation had met on the site since 1911, when they erected a large tent with wooden floor and sides as a place of worship. That winter, they covered the tent with shingles and put in windows with imitation coloured glass. According to the church's first organist, Mrs. Herbert Beeman, they had in addition to twelve choir boys "a fine choir outside the church—hundreds of little frogs croaking in the pools between the stumps." Construction commenced on the new church on February 11, 1913, and was completed in less than six months for about $11,000, including the cost of the land. Some years after the new church was completed, Mrs. Beeman obtained the tent, which was moved to the vacant land adjoining her little cottage at 42nd and Macdonald, several blocks to the southwest, where it served as the kindergarten run by her and her sister-in-law for many years.

Although St. Mary's Church appears to have been built all at once, it was in fact added to and modified several times over the six decades following its completion. Although current architectural and heritage orthodoxy states that additions to a building should be clearly distinguishable stylistically, the architects who worked on St. Mary's over the years evidently felt that any additions should enhance the Arts and Crafts style of the original building, which consisted of the nave and chancel only, with the characteristic bell-tower affixed

8. St. Mary's Church, at the corner of 37th and Larch.

above the west end. The side aisles, which have turned the nave's upper windows into a clerestory, were added by Sharp and Thompson in 1920; four years later, they added the parish hall immediately to the south of the church. In 1946-7, the noted local church architects Twizell and Twizell cut the church in two and spread it apart near its western end, to add another section; at the same time, the chancel was expanded eastward. The last major change to the building was the addition of a narthex in 1972 by architect William Rhone, to protect the body of the church from drafts and noise and to provide extra seating in a gallery above **(8)**.

In the late 1930s, Canon J.H. Craig argued that the building should be faced with brick or stone, and wanted at one point to build a new church on 41st Avenue; in the mid-1940s, there was a desire among a significant portion of the congregation to build a new stone church on the site. Part of the problem was aesthetics, but part was the overcrowding of the existing church. The latter problem was solved by the extension coordinated by R.P.S. Twizell, while the former, as the Reverend Dudley Kemp noted, ceased to be an issue for the congregation because "an English architect shortly after said publicly that wherever churches were built, and in whatever style, they should always be made of the local materials, which in the case of British Columbia is so predominantly wood."

9. (left) *The Sharp-designed house moved in the 1980s from the corner of 37th and Balsam to 2526 West 37th.*
10. (right) *The St. Mary's rectory, designed by G.L. Thornton Sharp, at the southwest corner of 37th and Larch.*

To the east of the church, on church property between it and Balsam Street, there were originally two houses. At the corner of Balsam Street was a simple, hipped-roof, half-timbered Arts and Crafts dwelling designed about 1914 by G.L. Thornton Sharp; it was moved in 1987 a block to the west and inserted onto the vacant lot at 2526 West 37th where it serves as a church residence and looks as if it has been since the creation **(9)**. A second, gambrel-roofed house on 37th Avenue stood immediately to the east of the main church; it was removed for a tennis court, which was replaced in 1951 by a gymnasium, lounge and classrooms, designed by Ross Lort. The formerly vacant lot at 2526 West 37th is one of two given to the church in 1920 by the Canadian Pacific Railway through the estates of the late Henry Cambie and John Hanbury. On the corner lot, at 2500 West 37th Avenue, Sharp designed a rectory, also in the Arts and Crafts style, which was built in 1920 **(10)**.

Continue walking west on 37th Avenue.

To the west of St. Mary's, the streetscape is no longer historically consistent, but there are nonetheless several interesting houses and a kind of small-town feel to the block—a combination of the buildings, landscaping, lack of curbs, gravel swales and street trees. Kitty-corner from the church, at 2503 West 37th Avenue, is the 1922 house built by A.J. Armstrong. It is a variation on the Craftsman-style Swiss Cottage, and for many years was the home of Dr. Watson Dykes, the health

11. The 1912 Pringle house at 2605 West 37th Avenue.

officer for the Municipality of Point Grey, who also had a private medical practice with an examining room in the house. In the 1950s, the house was a kindergarten operated by Mrs. Constance Grey. The odd-looking little mock-Tudor house at 2527 West 37th Avenue, probably dating from the 1930s, was moved onto its current lot in 1953.

The fine house behind the stone wall at 2605 West 37th Avenue was built early in 1912 for A. Pringle **(11)**. In the late 1920s, it was the Dorchester House School for Boys. It is a particularly well landscaped building, and shows all of the hallmarks of the Craftsman style in its mixing of stone and rough wood, leaded glass and exposed rafters. It is a tall house with a front gable; note the differences between it and the hipped-roof Arts and Crafts houses designed by George Thornton Sharp.

A new addition to the neighbourhood, but a building that is every bit as fine as the historic ones nearby, is the house built in the late 1980s at 2645 West 37th. Its curved dormers and sweeping roofline manage to reflect rural English influences (like the eyelid dormers of traditional cottages), but with a decidedly Japanese air. It was built on the site of a little cottage which, like the Smith house to its west, stood near the rear of its lot.

The much-modified, hipped-roof, Arts and Crafts house at 2677 West 37th Avenue was built about 1910 for the prominent surgeon Dr. Archibald Smith **(12)**. The fact that the house now stands at the

12. The 1910 Smith house at 2677 West 37th Avenue.

very back of its lot supports the supposition that it originally occupied the centre of a much larger piece of property, probably with a few hundred feet of frontage on both Whitehead and Taber roads (now 37th and 36th, respectively) east of Kaye Road (Trafalgar Street), which in 1910 had already been opened for some time. The house definitely antedates the formal subdivision of the blocks east of Trafalgar Street in 1911–12, and the enactment of standard set-back provisions in the Point Grey building by-law. It has evidently been divided into rooms and suites since the Second World War era.

Turn right at Trafalgar Street, then right again at 36th Avenue, and proceed eastward along 36th Avenue.

Trafalgar Street is one of the more significant roadways in this part of the city, as it is the dividing line between what were the CPR lands to the east (District Lot 526) and the privately owned District Lot 2027 to the west. District Lot 526, bounded roughly by English Bay, Ontario Street, Trafalgar Street and a ragged line at about Park Drive and 59th Avenue, was the major piece of the approximately six thousand acres granted to the CPR by the provincial government in the 1880s on the premise that it would assure the orderly development of a major city.

The earliest settlers in the Kerrisdale area bought in District Lot 2027, some acquiring estate-sized properties, while the CPR generally sold off and subdivided land piecemeal for housing lots, taking care not to flood the market and depreciate values. The subdivision in 1911 of what was then called Strathcona Heights—the blocks of 35th, 36th, and 37th to the east of the railway tracks, through which this walk will proceed—are a good example of controlled development, as the CPR had assured that water, electricity and transportation were readily available to prospective purchasers. The CPR was not interested in selling to homesteaders. (One of the few large properties sold by the CPR was the ten-acre "Shannon," to B.T. Rogers, a golfing partner of CPR western superintendent Richard Marpole.)

The northern end of Trafalgar Street, between English Bay and the city boundary at 16th Avenue, was originally called Boundary Road, as it was the boundary between the CPR lands and the privately owned (non-corporate) tracts to the west. At the turn of the century, the roadway continued south as little more than a trail, providing access to logging camps on Mackenzie Heights, and was known as Kaye Road after a local property owner; south of 41st

13. *A recently built house, at the northeast corner of 36th and Trafalgar, reflecting traditional designs without copying any particular house style.*

Avenue, the roadway followed the line of today's Macdonald Street, at the bottom of which were the McCleery, Magee and Mole farms, established on the Southlands flats since the 1860s. Prior to 1907, a number of the street names west of Larch Street duplicated names of streets elsewhere in the growing city, and consequently were changed to the names of famous English battles, Trafalgar being one.

At the northeast corner of 36th Avenue and Trafalgar is a very fine new Craftsman-inspired house with Japanese influences in its design, fence and landscaping, designed by Charles Moorhead and erected in 1991 **(13)**.

At this point, 36th Avenue used to be called Taber Road. The early houses on the block are the two near the middle: the 1912 house at 2599, built for J.M. Wedderburn and his sons David, John and Lawrence **(14)**; and the 1912 Craftsman house for William McNale at 2598 **(15)**. The Craftsman at 2606 West 36th was built for Joseph Rowlatt in 1919. The Wedderburn house is an upright, formal Vancouver Box, with half-timbering and shingling added by the builder to dress up what was really a simple shoebox. The McNale house is something of a clumsy Craftsman, with a gable on the side as in the traditional rural Swiss chalet. In good examples of the Craftsman style, the roof has a sheltering appearance, adding to the picturesque quality, and there is a lot of exposed woodwork, including heavy brackets, purlins and exposed rafters. The sense of texture and the honesty of materials in these fine wooden houses contributes to their charm.

14. The 1912 Wedderburn house, at 2599 West 36th.

15. *The 1912 McNale house, with expansive sideyard, at 2598 West 36th Avenue.*

Note also that on these old properties the houses are comparatively small and set in the middle of their gardens—these three old houses on West 36th have very substantial sideyards, and have the air of rural or small town, rather than urban, properties. In the last few years, following the demolition of houses such as these throughout this neighbourhood, the new construction has consistently been much bigger, the houses spreading across their lots and subtly removing one aspect of the local character that had little to do with architectural style.

East of Larch Street, 36th Avenue is lined with superb London plane trees (sycamores), with bark of a distinctive mottled colour, vivid in the dull winter light; in summer and fall, they cast an open, dappled shade, unlike the solid shade cast by horse chestnuts and some maples. In February, several of the gardens along these blocks have extensive beds of snowdrops and crocuses in blossom.

The house at 2303 West 36th Avenue, at the corner of Vine Street, was built in 1921 and is a classic example of a carpenter-built California Bungalow, probably from a stock house plan **(16)**. This type of simple, boxy house, with the main floor several steps above ground and an unfinished attic, is most often located on narrow, thirty-three-foot lots in districts of Vancouver such as Kitsilano or Douglas Park, where they were built by the thousands in the years around 1920, sometimes in rows. On this site, with sixty-six feet of frontage, the little house takes on a different character, with wide sideyards and fruit trees. It is quite a charming scene, but the house, being several steps

16. *The California Bungalow at 2303 West 36th Avenue.*

above the garden with comparatively few windows placed to allow anyone indoors to enjoy the verdure, does not really take advantage of its site. It is really just a little tract house plunked onto a lot but, like nearly all houses of the early years of this century, its wide front porch at least partially compensates for its inefficiencies and inadequacies. The California Bungalows viewed previously at the corner of Yew and 37th are more picturesque examples of the style.

On the north side, midway down the 2100-block, the last block before you arrive at Arbutus Street, there is a small concrete oval set into the ground at an angle, with "Ravine Park" affixed to it in iron letters. A pathway follows the course northward of one of the old salmon streams that once drained into English Bay. It winds through patches of damp shade and bright sun below the streets and houses and hurly-burly of the modern city, from 36th Avenue to 33rd. Worth exploring at any time of the year, it is especially enchanting in April and May, when many of the trees are in blossom. The old creek, now shackled by an underground conduit, is audible through the manhole covers along the pathway.

Cross the railway tracks, or perhaps use the crosswalk at 37th Avenue, and continue eastward up the 36th Avenue hill.

Note the particularly fine row of horse-chestnut trees on the curve along East Boulevard.

At this point, before the First World War, 36th was known as Centre Avenue—the centre of "Strathcona Heights." The Strathcona name appeared all over the Vancouver area, after Lord Strathcona of the Canadian Pacific Railway, but it is ironic that the name only stuck to the Strathcona district east of Chinatown (Chapter One)—land that was never owned by the CPR.

Many of the houses on the 2000-block West 36th are beautifully preserved examples of the "Swiss Cottage" Craftsman style, notable for their side gables, shingle covering, dormers on the fronts of the houses with little balconies that were originally used as sleeping porches, and leaded and bevelled glass on windows and doors. Of the houses completed in the spring of 1912, 2071, 2031, 2027 and 2019 are in excellent condition today. The architects, if there were any, are unknown; the houses were probably started on spec by an unknown builder and sold before completion (Municipality of Point Grey building permits no longer exist for the period before the autumn of 1912 and the new owners signed the water permits).

Note the fine Colonial Bungalow at 2063 West 37th; with its hipped roof, bellcast eaves, porch and small roof dormer, it bears the hallmarks of the style that began in India and evolved with local adaptations throughout the British Empire.

The Craftsman at 2049 was also completed in the spring of 1912; it was smaller than most of the others on the block, but was nevertheless superbly detailed, with extensive woodwork in its interior, and survived from 1918 until the late 1980s thanks to its owners, all members of the King family. As it had only two bedrooms and was too small to justify the contemporary lot value, it was modified and enlarged in 1990, with the addition of a second floor and a second front dormer, to the design of architect Rick Fearn. It is now a large, beautifully restored "new-old" heritage house, and won a City of Vancouver heritage award in 1991 **(17)**.

Proceed east along 36th Avenue, arriving eventually at the corner of Pine Crescent and 37th Avenue.

Note along the way the 1920s English cottage at the southeast corner of Maple and 36th; 1971 West 36th, which served as the St. Mary's

17. *The much-added-to King house, at 2049 West 36th Avenue.*

Church rectory in 1918; the Dutch Colonial Revival house at 1903 West 36th; the few old Craftsman houses; the 1970s cedar-sided modern houses landscaped with perennials at 1877-1845 West 36th; and the occasional developer-built "monster house" from the late 1980s.

Built up in the late 1920s and 1930s, Third Shaughnessy is one of the best examples in the city of a parklike garden landscape. Recently, to preserve its comparatively small houses from speculative redevelopment, the neighbourhood organized and obtained from the city a special zoning schedule that made it easier to renovate the existing houses than to demolish them. The theory behind the new zoning schedule was that the combination of established landscaping and architecture was crucial to the neighbourhood, and that when change came to a property it should ideally be more subtle and incremental than the catastrophic uprooting which characterizes new-house building.

While standing at the "five-points" corner of 37th, Pine Crescent and Angus Drive, observe the developers' houses of recent decades. At the northwest corner of 37th and Pine Crescent are two Vancouver Specials, built in the early 1970s and distinguishable from the thousands of identical houses elsewhere in the city only by their

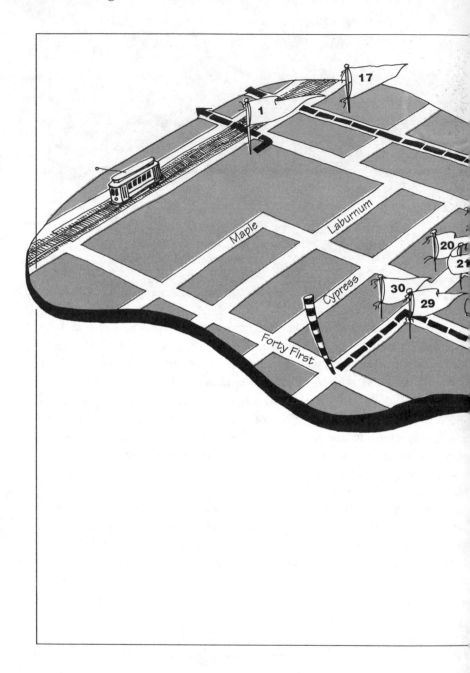

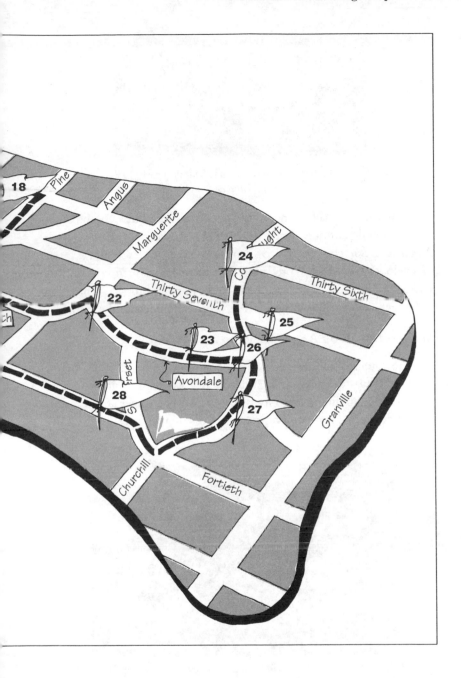

18. Wood-sided Vancouver Specials, built in the early 1970s at the corner of 37th and Pine Crescent.

wooden siding: usually Vancouver Specials are sided in a combination of stucco and "antique" brick veneer **(18)**. A few doors east on 37th Avenue from the corner of Angus Drive are two very large "Developer Georgians," predating the above-mentioned new zoning schedule; the fear locally was that these houses, and the large building to be seen later at 5669 Angus Drive, were harbingers of the future.

Walk south along Angus Drive to 38th Avenue.

The Dutch Colonial Revival-style Polson house at 5375 Angus Drive **(19)** was designed in 1926 by Henry Sandham Griffith, whose best-known building in the city is the 1912 office tower at the corner of Pender and Homer. Thomas C. Polson was president of the

19. The Polson house at 5375 Angus Drive, designed in 1926 by H.S. Griffith.

family-owned health food company called Dr. Middleton Food Products, manufacturers of Jo-To and Veg-O-Min, ironized whole-wheat flour and cereal products, Blue Ribbon White Bread, cookies, cakes and macaroons, which had its office and plant at 850 East Hastings (an advertisement for Jo-To appears in Chapter Two). City directories of the 1920s show that several Polsons in Vancouver were employed in some capacity or other with the firm.

The Cape Cod (sometimes called Colonial Revival) Halterman house at 5391 Angus Drive was designed in 1936 by C.B.K. Van Norman. He had a thriving and quite conservative residential practice in the city during the 1930s and 1940s, but is usually remembered for his 1950s buildings, including the Customs House and Burrard Building downtown, which brought the International style to Vancouver, and for his massive projects, including Park Royal Shopping Centre and Beach Towers. The Halterman house was built on one of the last available lots on this part of Angus Drive—even though the Great Depression almost stopped development elsewhere in the city, new house construction continued in this prosperous enclave.

The Dutch Colonial Revival Greenlees house at 5425 Angus Drive was designed in 1926 by Henry H. Simmonds. The firm of Hodgson and Simmonds designed the classically ornamented B.C. Electric Railway Company showrooms at Granville and Dunsmuir, until recently the location of Science World; Simmonds himself was

*20. The Atkinson house at 5475 Angus Drive, designed
in 1926 by Townley and Matheson.*

21. The Tudor Revival-style house by Charles Day at the southeast corner of 38th and Angus, photographed about 1930. (L. Frank photo, VPL 11271)

the architect of the Stanley Theatre. William Greenlees was a construction company president.

The Tudor Revival Atkinson house at 5475 Angus Drive, at the corner of 39th Avenue, was designed in 1926 by Townley and Matheson **(20)**. A few more of their Tudors appear later on this walk. The house was built by the noted carpenter and contractor W.J. Read, who often built Townley and Matheson plans.

At the southeast corner of 38th and Angus is a large Tudor Revival house designed for T.W. Greer by the architect J. Charles Day, and built in 1928 by A.Y. Thompson **(21)**. Another example of the collaboration of Day and Thompson appears later on the tour, but it is not in the Tudor Revival style.

Walk east on 38th Avenue, turn left at Marguerite, then right onto Somerset, and follow the curve of Avondale to the left.

While walking eastward along 38th, note the quality of design and finish of a number of builders' houses along the block and compare them with the architect-designed houses just viewed on Angus Drive.

Although very well finished and maintained, the Georgian Revival house at 1777 West 38th Avenue, unusual in the neighbour-

22. The Herger house at 1678 Somerset, in 1937. (L. Frank photo, VPL 11354)

hood because of its red-brick facing, is quite plain, without the gracious proportions seen in Georgians later in the walk; it was built in 1927 by the contractor D.R. Campbell for engineer Charles Beebe.

The house at 1749 West 38th is much more modest, and was a commissioned design from Charles Day for the speculative builder C.J. Phillips, who erected a large number of houses in this part of the city. Two other spec-built houses on the block are at 1735 and 1707 West 38th, built shortly after the area opened for development in 1926—like the Day/Phillips house, these buildings lack the sense of proportion and detailing of the better architect-designed houses.

Somerset Crescent and Avondale Crescent, with their narrow, curving roadways and variety of odd-shaped lots, offered more attractive and expansive building lots, resulting in some very distinguished homes. Probably the finest house on the street, and one of the two or three most elegant in the neighbourhood, is the W.E. Herger house at 1678 Somerset **(22)**, built in 1931 by the contractor S.W. Hopper, whose award-winning efforts twenty years earlier created an enclave of Japanese-influenced Craftsman houses on the 1600 and 1700 blocks of Dunbar Street in Kitsilano. (The City of Vancouver building permits registers of the time list only the owner and contractor, unlike the Municipality of Point Grey registers for the period before 1929—when Point Grey amalgamated with Vancouver—which also list the architect, if any. Thus, it is unknown whether Hopper or Herger employed an architect for this house.) It is a picturesque

23. The home of the architect Fred Townley, shortly after its completion in 1927.
(L. Frank photo, VPL 5054)

example of the English manor house, as if lifted from the pages of *Country Life* magazine.

Near the point where Avondale Crescent curves eastward from Somerset are two decidedly English houses—part of the supporting cast for the great houses of Third Shaughnessy. The brown shingle-covered home at 1691 Somerset was built in 1927 by the locally based contractor W.J. Read for the lumberman G.G.C. King. It is especially worth seeing in February, when the witch hazel near the front walk is in bloom. A few paces to the east is a fine Tudor designed in 1926 by the architect Frank Mountain (see below) and built by C.J. Phillips.

The enclave of four houses on Avondale, all by Townley and Matheson and constructed by W.J. Read, is the best set of their work surviving today. Although Townley and Matheson is best remembered for the austere, Moderne Vancouver City Hall, it worked in the 1920s in historical English styles, especially the Gothic, for buildings such as Tudor Manor and Point Grey School. Its residential work, especially in the 1920s, was equally English, conservative and picturesque.

Townley's own house, designed in 1926, is the shingle-covered English cottage with exceptionally steep roofline at 1636 Avondale **(23)**. An equally fine design is the brick-fronted Tudor for the

24. *The home of the architect R.M. Matheson, in the*
Norman style, at 5237 Connaught Drive.

McCleery family across the street at 1649 Avondale. With its connected garage and picturesque roofline, this is one of the more attractive and gracious houses in the area; it has recently been sensitively renovated and enlarged by the architect Ernest Collins.

Next door to the McCleery house at 1631 Avondale is another Townley and Matheson design of 1926, showing the narrow eaves, rounded bargeboard on the main gable and dropped side eaves reminiscent of the work of the English architect C.F.A. Voysey. It narrowly escaped demolition late in 1991 when a new owner wished to build a larger house in a non-traditional (for the area) style; the neighbours rallied to its protection, arguing that the intent of the area's new zoning schedule was to retain the existing houses as the key to preserving neighbourhood character.

The house at 1607 Avondale, also by Townley and Matheson and W.J. Read in 1926, was built for Hugh Dick. It illustrates the result of extensive and unsympathetic renovation over the years.

R.M. Matheson also built his own house nearby, in a traditional style. To see his house, erected in 1930, turn left at Connaught Drive and walk a block and a half to the north, to 5237 Connaught Drive **(24)**. It is a good example of the Norman Revival style, something of a rarity in Vancouver where other revival styles like the Tudor and the Georgian found much greater favour in the 1920s. Evidently, it was one of the first Normans in Vancouver, and inspired the appro-

25. The Willard house at 5326 Connaught Drive.

priately named C.B.K. Van Norman, who was then just starting out as an architect in Townley and Matheson's office, to design a number of them after he started his own practice later in the 1930s. The style is easily recognizable by such features as the hipped, steep roof, often with bellcast eaves, wall dormers, tall chimneys, and usually a tower, in some houses placed in the L formed by two wings of the house, in others dominating the front facade. The tower is sometimes conical and other times square, and often the house will have quoined corners. Another example of this style is the house at 5549 Cypress Street, a few blocks to the west.

Just to the north of the T of Avondale and Connaught is a very large white house, at 5326 Connaught, built on spec by F.M. Willard in 1926 **(25)**. With its white-painted cedar clapboards and shutters, it is an elaborate version of the American Colonial Revival or Cape Cod house of mid-1920s suburbia; its "blind Palladian" windows and loggia are also reminiscent of colonial times, being features of Georgian buildings of eighteenth-century America.

The house at 5376 Connaught Drive, designed in 1926 by the firm Benzie and Bow for a Major McAllister, is less interesting than its siting, with its long narrow garden to the south of the house. Because of these odd-shaped, non-rectilinear lots in parts of Third

26. A Ross Lort-designed Georgian at 1608 Avondale.

Shaughnessy, and the fact that the city's single-family zoning by-law was a straitjacket tailored to houses built on rectangular plots, houses such as this one were very difficult to renovate and upgrade without violating stipulations of the by-law; the area's new by-law mentioned above was specifically written to make these types of house the standard, and thus make them easier to maintain, renovate, and protect from demolition.

The J.G. Anderson house at 1608 Avondale is in the Georgian Revival style by the architect Ross Lort, and was constructed by E. Rodger in 1928 **(26)**. Ross Lort (1890-1968) was Samuel Maclure's partner at the end of the latter's career. Lort designed in a variety of styles, everything from the Moderne terminal building at the old airport and the International-style additions to the old Art Gallery, to the quaint "fairy cottages" at 587 King Edward and 3979 West 9th Avenue and the grand Spanish Colonial Revival folly "Casa Mia" on Southwest Marine Drive. His institutional work included York House School and the gymnasium for St. Mary's Church.

Walk south on Connaught Drive, then veer right onto Churchill Street.

One of the more active and talented builders of the period was Charles Woodburn, who erected four houses in a little enclave here:

27. *The house at 5584 Churchill, one of four spec-built houses by the contractor Charles Woodburn.*

5515 and 5550 Churchill in 1926, and 5516 and 5584 in 1928 **(27)**. All are boxy variations on the Tudor Revival style, where the house forms push out in all directions in a picturesque way from the central core—a style that began with the Gothic Revival in the mid-nineteenth century. Rough stucco forms most of the exterior finish and the houses feature interesting gables and complicated rooflines. Woodburn, who was architect, contractor and salesman, sometimes had his name emblazoned on a basement beam.

This type of builders' house is more typical of the blocks of Kerrisdale to the south, across 41st Avenue; there, the style evolved in the 1930s into an almost romantic triangular profile—wider at the base than at the eaves. The roofline on some houses extended to the lower floor in a graceful asymmetrical curve (a "cat-slide roof") that in some cases became a "flying buttress" false front containing an arched entranceway into the side garden. The picturesque evolution of these period houses became at its extreme the Hansel and Gretel style—fairy cottages, usually with Tudor detailing and steeply pitched roofs, a style that found its footing in the early 1920s in the fairyland of Los Angeles. The best local example of the style is a dozen blocks to the south: the 1923 Haley house at 1739 West 52nd Avenue.

On the southwest corner of 40th, Churchill, and Somerset is a splendid house with a steep Elizabethan turret roof above the front doorway, by the architects Benzie and Bow. It was designed in 1926 for A.B. Foster and sensitively enlarged in 1991. The copper beech in the front yard is one of the outstanding trees of the area. (As well as working in Third Shaughnessy in the 1920s, Benzie and Bow designed a number of houses in North Vancouver in the Tudor Revival and Arts and Crafts styles, including 1160, 1653 and 1753 Grand Boulevard.)

Turn west (right) onto 40th Avenue.

The two blocks of West 40th between Churchill Street and Angus Drive provide a good opportunity to view the works of Charles Day and Frank Mountain, two of the architects with busy residential practices and a specialty in period or revival-style architecture in Vancouver during the 1920s. Little personal information survives about either architect.

The exquisite Georgian Revival house at 1620 West 40th was designed by Charles Day in 1926 and built by A.Y. Thomson for J. Newbury **(28)**. The best Georgians are small, neat, symmetrical and rather plain, but have a beautiful sense of proportion in their windows, walls, shutters and roofs. With its wooden siding instead of stucco, this one is especially fine; note the curved balustrade on the porte-cochere.

Another Charles Day design is the Tudor Revival house at 1644 West 40th, built in 1927 for R.B. Harvey by C.J. Phillips. Phillips

28. A very fine little Georgian with battens and shutters, designed in 1926 for J. Newbury by the architect Charles Day.

also built the Georgian at 1631 West 40th, which was designed by Frank Mountain and is the only example of his work that is not in the Tudor style. The house at 1655 is another spec-built Charles Woodburn house.

On the next block are three Frank Mountain-designed Tudors: 1742 and 1776 were both built by C.J. Phillips in 1927, while 1757 was built in 1926 by the contractor Archibald Sullivan. One other house is worth noting: the Georgian at 1758 West 40th was designed for Dr. Freeze in 1926 by H.S. Griffith, whose other known effort in this neighbourhood, mentioned above, was in the Dutch Colonial Revival style.

Note the mushroom-shaped, contorted Camperdown Elm at the southeast corner of 40th and Marguerite, another of the outstanding trees in the area.

The Tudor at the corner of Angus and 40th was designed in 1928 by B.C. Palmer for Mrs. Edward Douglas, the widow of one of the partners of the Kelly-Douglas wholesale grocery business **(29)**. Frank Douglas, the original partner of Robert Kelly, drowned in a Klondike-era shipwreck; his brother Edward came to Vancouver from Minnesota, joined the firm, and provided for the widow. Edward Douglas died in 1927. Bernard Cuddon Palmer was consulting architect for the Lions Gate Bridge, and designed the log Craftsman "Fairweather" on Bowen Island for the Rogers family, as well as the Spanish Colonial Revival "Rio Vista" on Southwest Marine Drive,

29. *The Douglas house, designed by Bernard Palmer, at 5610 Angus Drive.*

*30. The Montgomery house at 5629 Angus Drive, designed in 1926
by Honeyman and Curtis.*

with its unique Pompeian pool and spectacular gardens by Raoul Robillard, for Harry Reifel. These vastly different houses were both designed about 1930; "Rio Vista" antedates (and is much more finely proportioned and detailed than) Ross Lort's "Casa Mia," built for Harry Reifel's brother George, by two years.

Palmer's other known efforts include the finishing touches on "Rosemary," a Maclure and Fox design at 3689 Selkirk Street in First Shaughnessy, and the completion in the mid-1920s of "Shannon" at 57th and Granville, designed for B.T. Rogers by Somervell and Putnam.

Turn south (left) onto Angus Drive.

Flanked by inferior builders' Tudors, the nicest house on the block of Angus between 40th and 41st Avenue is the D.S. Montgomery home at 5629 Angus Drive, designed by Honeyman and Curtis in 1926 and built by Stewart and Coltart **(30)**. It is also a Tudor Revival house, but, like the Palmer-designed house across the street, has a sense of softness and texture not unlike G.L. Thornton Sharp's Arts and Crafts house near St. Mary's Church. Honeyman and Curtis's best-known residential design in Vancouver is the very large Craftsman-style Logan house at 2530 Point Grey Road in

Kitsilano, now much modified but still retaining its original character. Like Benzie and Bow, Honeyman and Curtis did a lot of its residential work in the City of North Vancouver.

At 5669 Angus Drive there stood a particularly fine combination of 1935 Georgian house and clipped landscaping with tied columnar cedars, all of which was demolished and dug up in the spring of 1989. This loss, coupled with the scale and design of the new house, helped to prompt the local owners to petition the city for a new zoning schedule that would protect the old architecture and garden ambience of the area.

North Vancouver City

1 - 1 ½ HOURS

A trip on the SeaBus across Burrard Inlet allows you to approach the City of North Vancouver in its best "historic" manner—by water. The SeaBus leaves from the former CPR station at the foot of Seymour Street in downtown Vancouver—a few blocks to the west of the old North Vancouver ferry terminal at the foot of Columbia—and crosses the harbour in a few minutes to a terminus a stone's throw to the west of the old city wharf at the foot of Lonsdale. From the SeaBus, there is still a good view of historic North Vancouver: the Wallace Shipyards to the east of Lonsdale, dating in part from the First World War years; old Ferry Number 5 (for the past thirty-five years doing duty as the Seven Seas seafood restaurant) moored at the foot of Lonsdale; the Cates shipyard just to its west;

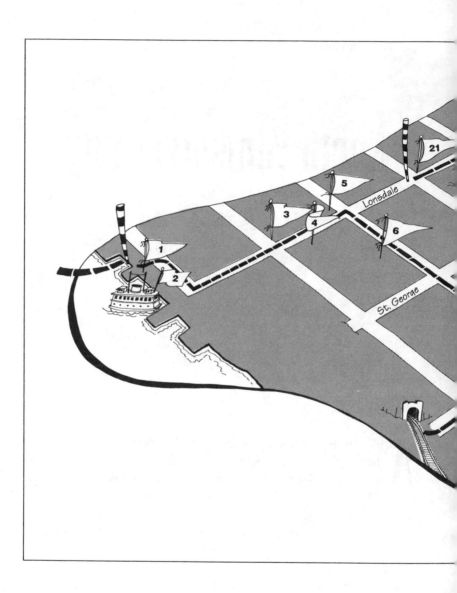

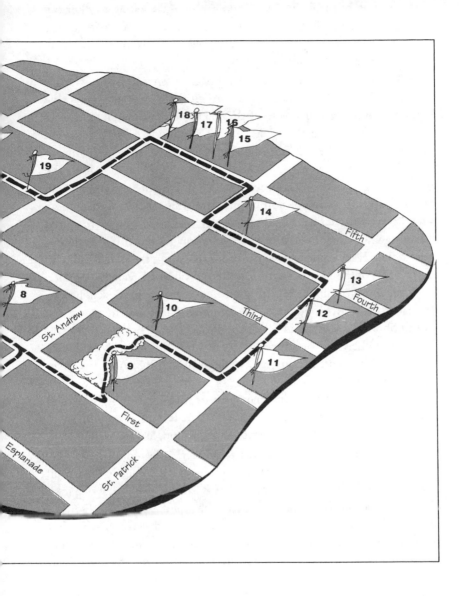

and the small buildings nearby, clustered around what was the transportation hub of the early city. It takes some imagination to filter out the newer, tall buildings, and to focus selectively only on that little area which was a compact town, separated by bush from the rest of the metropolis in the years before the 1940s.

While on the SeaBus and still a good distance from the North Shore, it is worth indulging in two other pieces of "selective focusing" to imagine that side of the inlet as it was in an even earlier era. Some distance to the west (left) of the modern jumble around Lonsdale Quay—the "Q" sign next to the "Cates" sign—a sharp eye will pick out the twin spires of St. Paul's Church at Ustlawn, the native village on the shoreline. The church is the only surviving building from the model community and mission established there after 1860 by the Roman Catholic Church; although the twin-spired facade facing Vancouver is a 1909 addition to the original single-spired church, its nave dates from 1886, making it the oldest building on this part of the North Shore. To the east of North Vancouver City, on a site now occupied by the grain elevators of the Saskatchewan Wheat Pool, was Moodyville, the original white settlement on the North Shore. Established in 1862, the Pioneer Mills sawmill there was the first lumber mill on Burrard Inlet; it got the name Moodyville from Sewell Prescott Moody, who bought it in 1865. Although over the next thirty years it was the centre of a significant community, with the large houses of the mill managers occupying the high ground above, it became outmoded and was closed in 1901. Fifteen years later, the abandoned mill buildings burnt to the ground, leaving no trace.

The original ferry service across Burrard Inlet connected New Brighton—now New Brighton Park near the Pacific National Exhibiton—with Moodyville, and was started by "Navvy Jack" Thomas in 1866. New Brighton was the point where the Douglas Road, cleared by the Royal Engineers northward from New Westminster, reached tidewater; for a brief period in the late 1860s and 1870s, it was a fashionable little watering hole and resort for residents of New Westminster and (not least because of Sewell Moody's teetotal beliefs) Moodyville.

Development in North Vancouver shifted west from Moodyville after the mill closed in 1901. The District of North Vancouver had already been incorporated for ten years, as had the North Vancouver Land and Improvement Company, with principal shareholders in England and a locally based manager, Edward Mahon. (Even at the turn of the century, though, North Vancouver was still far enough from the centres of population to be considered a suitable site for a resort hotel, which Peter Larson erected on the Esplanade in 1902. Although the Hotel North Vancouver burned to the ground in 1929, part of its garden retaining wall can still be seen, at 166 Esplanade West.) Completing the extinction of Moodyville, the post office moved west to the Lonsdale area following the closure of the mill.

In 1903, the North Shore came into its own with the incorporation of the North Vancouver Ferry and Power Company, established with a combination of English and local capital under the direction of Alfred St. George Hamersley. The assurance of regular transportation and the general economic buoyancy of the times prompted a land boom in North Vancouver, which continued unabated until the international financial collapse in 1913. In the midst of the boom, on May 13, 1907, the City of North Vancouver incorporated itself.

Because of the unsteady provincial economy and erratic population and business growth in the years after 1913, and the enormous amount of developable land, there was little chance that North Vancouver would develop into a concentrated city—the kind of development that creates towns with a heritage or period aspect to them. Indeed, the legacy of so much land speculation is still very evident in the patchy development of the Lower Lonsdale area, and in isolated commercial buildings elsewhere such as the 1912 Dundarave Block at 16th and Lonsdale, a long hike to the north. It is interesting that so many of the very early residential and commercial buildings have survived the boom years since the end of the Second World War, although the reason is apparent—the automobile.

By the 1920s, although the ferries between North Vancouver and downtown were relatively efficient and could even accommodate automobiles, many suburbanites were being attracted to the North Shore by the possibility of commuting directly to their jobs by car. The first bridge to cross the inlet was the low-level "steeplechase" to the east of the modern Second Narrows Bridge. Opened in 1925, it was intended mainly for trains but accommodated toll-paying cars on its outrigger trestles; everyone had to wait when the bascule span opened to allow freighters through. Nevertheless, it was a tolerable situation, at least until 1930, when a freighter took out the main span. As the Second Narrows Bridge Company was suffering the effects of the Great Depression, it announced that it would be unable to make the necessary repairs, prompting a Vancouver alderman, who had collected nearly two thousand unusable toll tickets from unhappy former commuters, to slander it and its directors. The resulting legal action dragged on unresolved until June, 1934, when the company finally reopened the bridge, and the plaintiffs decided to drop their action.

In the prosperous atmosphere of the early 1950s, all forms of public transit were considered to be expendable, as almost everyone could afford a private automobile (and wartime gas rationing was already a distant memory). The B.C. Electric Railway Company ceased operation of its North Vancouver streetcar lines in the late 1940s and in the early 1950s began to dismantle its extensive interurban railway network. In its attitude towards its transit service, the BCER's actions dovetailed neatly with provincial government highway-building policy: additions to Greater Vancouver's road system during the fifties included the Oak Street Bridge and Highway 99 connection to the American border and, most significantly for North Vancouver, the construction of a new Second Narrows Bridge, none of which contained any provision for rail transit. With the impending demise of the interconnecting land-transit system at both of its termini, the North Vancouver ferry system ceased operation in 1958.

In the 1950s and 1960s, real-estate development in North Vancouver was attracted to areas more easily served by, and accessible to, the private automobile, leading to the development of the vast hinterland that had been left untouched by the streetcar era; meanwhile, the old buildings of Lower Lonsdale remained relatively ignored. Now, thirty-five years later, with traffic becoming a nightmare throughout the Lower Mainland, developers are perceiving a market for buildings in locations serving more urban lifestyles, reflected in the recent developments at Lonsdale Quay. These are the harbingers of a bright and booming future for the City of North Vancouver. Ironically, although the ghosts of the original real-estate developers of the turn of the century will finally see their dreams

The Pacific Great Eastern station at the foot of Lonsdale, about 1915. The large building on the hillside is the Saint Alice Hotel. (Photographer unknown, NSMA 1479)

come true, it will probably mean the loss of much of their legacy—the quaint and historic buildings of Lower Lonsdale, within a few blocks of the Quay.

Another piece of the old North Shore transportation network that has vanished is the Pacific Great Eastern Railway station, which used to stand on the west side of Lonsdale right at the shoreline. It was erected in 1913 as the terminus of the railway system that would, according to its promoters, funnel the wealth of northern British Columbia through the port of North Vancouver. However, because of the Depression and subsequent war, the PGE became the railway "from nowhere to nowhere," otherwise known as the Please Go Easy, the Prince George Eventually, and the Province's Greatest Expense. Before its collapse, it did manage, in 1914, to commence service between Lonsdale and West Vancouver and eventually reached Whytecliffe. As a piece of local transportation it survived until 1928, in competition from downtown Vancouver with the older West Vancouver ferry service; as a provincially owned crown corporation it finally made it to Squamish, and then Prince George, in the 1950s. The station building was moved in 1971 from the foot of Lonsdale to Mahon Park on West 16th Street; today, the passenger terminus of B.C. Rail, the corporate successor to the PGE, is at the foot of Pemberton in North Vancouver District.

Walk through Lonsdale Quay and exit; proceed up the lane west of Lonsdale to Esplanade; turn right and walk to Lonsdale.

As you exit Lonsdale Quay, there is an excellent view of the Cates ship-repair facility **(1)**.

The little hipped-roofed building in the lane, now called Lonsdale Antiques, was built about 1905 as the office of the North Vancouver Cartage Company, which had its stables several blocks away on East 4th Street. As telephone service began in North Vancouver in 1906, this arrangement probably worked quite well. According to the City of North Vancouver heritage inventory, the tiny cartage office was a common political meeting place, presumably not for wildly popular political figures. Originally, the building faced onto Lonsdale, but was moved about 1920 to the back of the lot to make room for a larger edifice.

From the corner of Lonsdale and Esplanade, there is an excellent view southward to the City of Vancouver and to old Ferry Number 5, built in 1941, and both the last built and the last surviving of the end-to-end-loading North Vancouver ferries. Its capacity was six hundred passengers and thirty vehicles **(2)**. It is worthwhile walking a half-block towards the water on Lonsdale to see the line incised in the pavement marking the 1905 shoreline, and noting the amount of harbour filling that has taken place in the past eighty-five years—a phenomenon not unique to North Vancouver by any means, as Vancouver's waterline has been marching northward at an even greater rate.

1. The Cates ship-repair facility beside Lonsdale Quay.

2. Old Ferry Number 5 at the foot of Lonsdale.

The block of Lonsdale between Esplanade and 1st Street contains the greatest surviving cluster of North Vancouver's commercial heritage buildings. Perhaps not surprisingly, the most important building historically is the least distinguished architecturally—the Syndicate Block at 51-59 Lonsdale (the northwest corner of Lonsdale and Esplanade), dating from 1903. It is doubly important because it is not only the oldest commercial block on the North Shore, it was actually the first one built **(3)**. Originally, it housed the grocery store of J.A. McMillan and the North Vancouver post office, which had just moved from Moodyville; another early tenant was the North Shore's first newspaper, the *Express*, and dances and meetings were held in the upstairs hall. The noted land developer J.C. Keith, whose name is commemorated in Keith Road, was one of the members of the builders' syndicate—the Western Corporation.

Of all of the buildings in Lower Lonsdale, the Syndicate Block is probably most at risk, because of its strategic location (the reason it was built there ninety years ago), its modest wood-framed construction, and its somewhat shabby condition. It sold in the spring of 1992 for $2.4 million—an indication that, without some intervention by the City of North Vancouver in the form of heritage "sticks and carrots," it may soon be the object of a demolition application.

The two buildings on the east side of Lonsdale in the same block date from 1910 and are much more substantial, giving them a better chance of survival in the 1990s real-estate jungle, and demonstrating just how far North Vancouver progressed in the seven years after the construction of the Syndicate Block. Farthest south is the Aberdeen

3. The Syndicate Block, about 1905 (Photographer unknown, NSMA 2777)

Block, at 78-90 Lonsdale, by the architects Mills and Hutton; it was originally known as the Keith Block, after the above-mentioned J.C. Keith, explaining the "K" on a shield above the building's main entrance **(4)**. It was the location of some of the prominent operations of the new city, including the Post Office (in 1911 and 1912, after it had moved from the Syndicate Block), the B.C. Electric Railway Company, and the city administration. One of its current tenants, Paine Hardware, has become renowned throughout the Lower Mainland as an old-fashioned hardware store where you can buy, for example, the single screw you need rather than an expensive plastic pack of a dozen or so of them.

The three-storey building to the north, stepped a storey higher due to the rising ground, is the Bank of Hamilton Building, by the same architects as the Aberdeen Block. Dating from a time when banks sought classical design motifs to reflect their permanence (which, in the case of the ill-fated Bank of Hamilton, was unwarranted), the building has pilasters with Ionic capitals; one of its concessions to modernity was a passenger elevator, the first of its kind on the North Shore. The Bank of Hamilton had its original North Vancouver location across the street in the Keith Block, which has

4. (left) *The entrance to the Aberdeen Block.*
5. (right) *The 1908 Keith Block at 1st and Lonsdale.*

facades facing both Lonsdale and 1st Street, and was erected in 1908
(5). The building on the northwest corner of 1st and Lonsdale, with a
street address of 101–109 Lonsdale, dates from 1904, and was called
the Beasley Block, with a doctor's office above and a drugstore con-
veniently on the main floor; like the Syndicate Block a block to the
south, it was built by the Western Corporation. Originally, it was
covered in drop siding and, with its false front and corner entry,
looked a lot like the Arbutus Grocery in Kitsilano (Chapter Five).

Walk east on 1st Street.

With its patchy development and vacant lots, the block of 1st
Street immediately east of Lonsdale is one of the monuments to land
speculation on the North Shore. The biggest building is the Mount
Crown Block, designed in 1911 by the architects Dalton and Eveleigh
with two floors of bay-windowed apartments above ground-floor retail
space. Dalton and Eveleigh were associated with F.M. Rattenbury in
the design and construction of the Court House (now the Art Gallery)
in Vancouver, and designed the Royal Bank at Homer and Hastings
and the Davis Chambers (now demolished) on Hastings west of
Seymour. Although the Mount Crown Block's cornice has been

removed, and the main-floor shops have been renovated in an unsympathetic fashion, the building nevertheless shows the trend of development that was interrupted by the 1913 crash. Thanks to the crash, streets of apartments were never built, and there remain a few old houses on properties almost like old orchards: an old builder's house deteriorating slowly into a willow grove at 126 East 1st Street, and the Falcioni house at 168 East 1st Street, built in 1908 for a labourer at the nearby shipyards and his wife, a packer in a candy factory. These are examples of a type of house, originally built for working-class owners, that was eliminated from downtown Vancouver by the 1920s, but has survived for an additional lifetime in economically depressed Lower Lonsdale.

It is worth mentioning the cottage that stood across the street from the two old houses on the north side until 1992, when it was moved to Lynn Headwaters Park. The cottage is a B.C. Mills, Timber and Trading Company "Model J" prefabricated house, placed on the lot in 1908 by Captain Henry Pybus, the captain of the *Empress of Japan*. Pybus owned property all over the Lower Mainland, and lost nearly all of it in the crash of 1913. In the generations since, the little house sat within a stone's throw of bustling Lonsdale, gradually deteriorating, its lot a thicket of blackberry canes **(6)**.

The block of 1st Street farther to the east, between St. Georges and St. Andrews, has none of the forlorn air that still haunts the 100

6. The Pybus house, as it appeared in its original location
on 1st Street in the spring of 1992.

*7. Harbour Manor at 250-254 East 1st, the first apartment
building in North Vancouver.*

block, and is a bustling little industrial area of a type not often seen
any more in the Lower Mainland—loading bays open directly onto
the street and the sidewalks and streets are shared by pedestrians,
goods and vehicles. In the middle of the block is "Harbour Manor,"
built in 1910 at 250-254 East 1st, which was actually the first apartment block in North Vancouver, but has in recent years been
restored and adapted to the changed nature of the street with a conversion of the second floor apartments into offices **(7)**. With its four
bay windows, and the date of construction and building name affixed
to a curved parapet, the building is a nice contrast with the spare
designs of the other buildings that form the block's streetwall.
Immediately to its east, and tucked into a green oasis behind a very
large alder, is the last house on that block, and one of the older houses
left in North Vancouver—the Emery house **(8)**. Built in 1906 for a

8. The Emery house, which sits at the back of its lot, is most visible from the lane.

man who became a North Vancouver city councillor the following year, the house still has its original intricate fretwork and fishscale shingling in its gable, visible if you peer through the screen of foliage in front of the house.

It is worth walking down the hill on St. Andrews Avenue and crossing Esplanade to get a closer look at the shipyard buildings and to see, to the west of the foot of the street, the portal of the Vancouver Harbour Commissioners' terminal railway tunnel with "V H C" and the date emblazoned onto its concrete face. Opened by Viscount Willingdon, the governor general, in 1929, the tunnel moved railway traffic efficiently along the waterfront; PGE trains then used the Second Narrows Bridge to link with Vancouver lines.

The shipyards themselves were established about 1906 along the North Vancouver waterfront by Alfred Wallace, who for the previous fifteen years had been building boats in a set of floating sheds on False Creek known as Wallace's Marine Ways. Initially, Wallace specialized in the so-called Columbia River salmon-fishing boats which, with their moulded hulls, gradually replaced the flat-bottomed skiffs typically used on the Fraser River and elsewhere; when completed and awaiting sale, his boats were tied in strings, nose to tail, to the original Granville Street trestle. In 1900, to build the steamer *Kestrel*, Wallace received the first Dominion government contract ever awarded in Vancouver. Another shipbuilder on False Creek who moved to North Vancouver was Charles Cates, mentioned above, whose Beach

Avenue shipyard occupied the land under the north piers of the Burrard Street Bridge.

The buildings on Esplanade east of Lonsdale all date from the years after 1911, when a fire destroyed Wallace's original buildings. Under Wallace's son Clarence, the business became known as Burrard Dry Dock, and bought out a number of local firms, including J. Coughlan and Sons, which in 1919 had secured from the Dominion government a subsidy to build a dry dock for Vancouver harbour. Burrard Dry Dock later became known as Burrard Yarrows, following its purchase in 1946 of the Yarrows shipyard in Esquimalt. Clarence Wallace himself was the province's lieutenant governor from 1950 to 1955. Most recently known as Versatile Pacific, the shipyards have been plagued by lack of demand and on-again-off-again government contracts; in the near future, the industrial flavour of the site may disappear entirely, submerged under a tsunami of waterfront condos.

A sharp contrast to the little factories of the 200-block of East 1st, and the sprawling industrial complex to the south, is the pastoral gardener's cottage at 364 East 1st Street, a half-block to the east of St. Andrews **(9)**. Built in 1904 as part of the Hamersley estate, the cottage is a clapboard structure with a simple fore-and-aft pitched roof, made elegant by its wraparound porch and the large, open-sawn fretwork brackets on its posts. It is set about a hundred yards south of the Hamersley mansion, originally known as "Langton Lodge," and is thus one of the rareties of middle-class Vancouver—a purpose-built servant's dwelling. "Langton Lodge," the cottage, and sundry ancillary

9. The Hamersley gardener's cottage at 364 East 1st.

buildings and stables occupied the high ground of a property which ran from the waterfront to 3rd Street between St. Andrews and St. Patricks; in addition, Hamersley owned a considerable amount of real estate elsewhere in North Vancouver and, as mentioned above, developed the ferry service to Vancouver which was intended to ensure a ready market for North Vancouver property.

As a young man, Hamersley had been educated at Marlborough, England, and left in his twenties for military service in New Zealand, from where he immigrated to Vancouver in 1888. Before moving to North Vancouver, Hamersley had lived on prestigious Seaton Street, now Hastings Street west of Burrard, and had been Vancouver's city solicitor; his private interests included the chairmanship of the Union Steamship Company at its inception in 1890. A handsome and aristocratic Englishman, he evidently left his job after a falling out with the mayor, Fred Buscombe, who made his living selling plumbing fittings through a store known as Skinner's; according to one of the few stories surviving about his time in Vancouver, Hamersley, after being criticized by the mayor during a 1904 council meeting, strode from the meeting, announcing that he would not be abused by "a mere purveyor of chamber pots." Around that time, he was trying his hand at hop farming near Agassiz but, as was the case with his investments and estate in North Vancouver, he soon lost interest. In 1906, he returned to Oxfordshire in England and the family home. From 1910 to 1918, he was Conservative member of parliament for his mid-Oxfordshire district. He died in 1929 in his seventy-ninth year.

Walk north through Hamersley Park to 2nd Street, then walk east.

The little park immediately to the west of the gardener's cottage lacks the estate character of the original property, but does contain two very old wild cherry trees, probably dating to 1904 and the establishment of the estate. A pathway meanders through a mixture of native and introduced plants and climbs the bank at the north end of the park, winding through the trees above the cottage before reaching 2nd Street. Immediately across the street is the mansion "Langton Lodge," which is one of the most solidly built structures on the entire

10. "Langton Lodge," as it appears from 2nd Street.

Lower Mainland **(10)**. Above its foundations of cut granite blocks are brick and concrete walls, in some places as much as nineteen inches thick—not surprisingly, it took two years to complete. However, the house has a picturesque and woodsy quality, appropriate to what was once a rural setting, due to its Arts and Crafts design and the shingles covering all those hard surfaces. It is amazing that Hamersley abandoned the place after putting so much investment into it, but the City of North Vancouver has exacted a certain revenge by mispelling his name on the plaque in front of the gardener's cottage.

A half-block to the east of "Langton Lodge" is a much more modest suburban property—the Jones house at 408 East 2nd Street, built in 1906 for a conductor on the B.C. Electric Railway. As is evident from the battens on the building's main floor, it is a B.C. Mills, Timber and Trading Company prefab. Specifically, it is a Model "LL," with a wall dormer on the west (left) side for the staircase ascending to three upstairs bedrooms; the bathroom and kitchen were at the rear of the main floor, behind a fine dining room and parlour with a bay window **(11)**. Measuring twenty and one-half feet wide and thirty-three feet deep, the house was designed for narrow city

11. The Jones house, a restored Model "LL" BCMT&T prefab erected in 1906.

lots, and Mr. Jones bought it unassembled for $770. It has recently been restored, and infill units have been built in the back yard to provide a bonus in return for the heritage retention.

Walk north on St. Patricks Avenue.

These blocks of North Vancouver have scattered examples of pre-World War One houses, all of which reflect a construction and design quality vastly superior to the houses built in more recent decades, such as one example beside the Jones house, at the northeast corner of 2nd and St. Patricks—a classic 1960s side-by-side Vancouver Special duplex, with little wrought-iron balconies on the second floor above garage doors.

In between the eras of the Jones house and the Vancouver Specials was the Second World War, during which North Vancouver was a centre of heavy industry, especially shipbuilding at the Burrard Dry Dock a few blocks away. Accordingly, in 1941, several hundred small houses were built on vacant lots in the area for the workmen drawn to the industrial jobs nearby. The workers' houses were the ultimate in affordability: four or six rooms on one floor, a tiny front stoop several steps above ground level, and a simple side-gabled roof. The construction, which was designed and supervised by the architectural firm of McCarter and Nairne (responsible, in palmier times, for the Marine Building), included a few hundred detached houses in this area, and two large bachelors' halls, holding ninety men each, erected at the corner of 3rd and St. Georges.

The two houses at 240 St. Patricks and 402 East 3rd Street are good examples of wartime housing, and have not been modified significantly from the original design **(12)**. Demolitions for newer houses and for apartment redevelopment have eliminated many of these houses, and certainly any sense of a streetscape of wartime housing in this part of North Vancouver has disappeared. A more intact enclave of wartime housing in the Lower Mainland is Burkeville on Sea Island near the Vancouver International Airport, erected in 1943 for the workers at a nearby Boeing Aircraft plant and their families.

Compare these two wartime houses visible on the walk up St. Patricks with the house at 341 St. Patricks, which is a postwar "starter house"—the kind built throughout the Lower Mainland for returned servicemen and their new families. The design of 341 St. Patricks features a hipped roof, rather than a gabled one, and has the characteristic stucco on the main floor above wide bevelled siding at the basement level, typical of so many thousands of houses from the 1940s and 1950s.

12. *A surviving example of wartime housing at 402 East 3rd Street.*

13. The Henderson house at 405 East 4th Street.

Just east of St. Patricks on 4th Street is one of the fine houses from North Vancouver's first flush of prosperity. Built in 1910 for a civil engineer named Arthur Henderson, the house at 405 East 4th is a very good local variation on the Shingle-style houses built in the eastern United States in the 1880s **(13)**. Its gambrel roof with the "Dutch kick" flare at the bottom—a feature revived from the Dutch colonial dwellings of seventeenth- and eighteenth-century New York State—is very typical of that style. The Henderson house is interesting as well because it is one of a minority of houses from that period in the Lower Mainland that were actually customized to take advantage of an unusual site or a particular view. In this case, the porch and bay window were angled to take advantage of the view to the southwest. By comparison, most houses were stock designs which, in many cases, actually turned their backs to spectacular views; it is much the same with builders' houses today.

Walk west on 4th Street.

The streetscape in the block of 3rd Street between St. Patricks and St. Andrews is something of a classic in its own right, being a combination of side-by-side and up-and-down duplexes of the 1950s and 1960s. Many of these demonstrate how builders in that period took the elements of the International style, illustrated in major downtown structures such as the Burrard Building and the B.C. Electric (Hydro) Building, and created a cheap vernacular style that nevertheless appeared modern. These buildings, along with "walk-up" apartments throughout the Lower Mainland, prove that, while it was difficult to build a bad Queen Anne, it was easy to build a bad International-style building.

As examples of this builders' vernacular, three duplexes are worth a glance while hurrying by. The flat-roofed building at 376–378 East 4th has an austere stucco facade with one three-paned aluminum window on each floor, separated vertically from the one below by a spandrel consisting of vertically nailed shiplap strips. Number 366–368 East 4th is a flat-roofed side-by-side duplex, with stucco above the basement level of bevelled siding, as in the house previously seen at 341 St. Patricks. Yet another variation is 316 East 4th, a tall, three-storey, flat-roofed apartment on a wide lot; it has vertically nailed shiplap that, with the aluminum windows, form horizontal bands

14. 316 East 4th Street, regrettably a characteristic apartment building of the postwar period.

across the stucco-covered facade **(14)**. The choice of flat roofs on small residential buildings in a district with about eighty inches of rain a year shows the extent to which fashion had won over practicality.

Turn north (right) at St. Andrews, then west (left) at East 5th Street.

By comparison with the post-World War Two streetscape on 4th Street, this part of 5th Street—at least on its north side—is Edwardian. One of the most attractive houses in this part of North Vancouver is at the northeast corner of 5th and St. Andrews—a Tudor Revival building from before the First World War. (A much better Tudor, dating from 1908, stands a half-block to the east at 387 East 5th Street; it now faces south into the alley between 4th and 5th, as the original property was broken up years before.)

Until a few years ago, before the 1912 house at 240 East 5th was demolished, there was an intact Edwardian streetscape of five houses on the north side of 5th west of St. Andrews. Those that remain include the Edwardian Builder-style Ward house at 246-248 East 5th Street, built in 1914; it has the cyclops dormer set in a hipped roof typical of houses built in Vancouver in the first decade of this century **(15)**. To its west is a 1911 house built for Fred King **(16)**. The two houses at 232 and 234, the latter of which has been stuccoed, were designed by the architect M.J. Beaton in 1911 and built as a speculative investment.

A contrast with these vertical Edwardian houses is the thirties bungalow at 222 East 5th Street—an evolution of the Cape Cod builder's house of suburbia—which is intact except for aluminum windows on its front elevation **(17)**. The elements making up this superb period package are those advertised in house-and-garden magazines of the Depression years: a modest-sized single-storey house on a fairly expansive lot, well landscaped with a rockery and clipped shrubs; hipped roof; wide bevelled siding; above the doorway a semicircular pediment incorporated into the eave above the front door, supported by the sort of ogee brackets that made their first appearance supporting the hipped roofs on Italianate villas in the 1850s; and, especially, octagon windows. Used as a feature window to light the entranceways and hallways of little houses, the octagon or diamond window (the latter often made more decorative with clear leaded glass) was in fashion for twenty-five years commencing about 1935. The arched pediment above the front door was a common feature of Dutch Colonial Revival houses of the late 1920s.

Another curious period house is the Streamline Moderne duplex at the northeast corner of 5th and St. Georges **(18)**. Like the duplexes

15. (top, left) *The Ward house at 246-248 East 5th Street.*
16. (top, right) *The 1911 King house at 244 East 5th Street.*
17. (bottom) *Cape Cod meets suburbia in the 1930s—the house at 222 East 5th Street.*

18. The Streamline Moderne duplex at the corner of 5th and St. Georges.

viewed earlier on 4th Street, this house demonstrates how unsuccess-fully, in the hands of most builders with small budgets, the post–World War Two commercial architectural styles adapted to small-home design.

There is a good view, looking along St. Georges Avenue, of St. Andrews Church some blocks to the north. St. Andrews was origi-nally a Presbyterian congregation founded in 1904 on 6th Street; in 1912, it built the current Gothic Revival building, whose spire is so visible from many locations in North Vancouver, to the design of the architects Alexander and Brown.

Walk south on St. Georges Avenue to 3rd Street, turn right, and walk west to Lonsdale.

The three houses numbered 154, 152 and 146 East 3rd Street were built about 1905 **(19)**. Number 154 is a square, Georgian-influenced building, erected for the Hughes family, as was number 152, which was rented to the owner of a grocery store on Lonsdale Avenue. The latter is the best preserved of the three houses—a simple, gabled house with an elegantly proportioned porch and fine fretwork detailing and shingling. However, the house at 146 East 3rd is the most interesting of the three; although now blanketed in stucco and robbed of much of its original detailing, its Queen Anne origins show through in the double bay windows on the front and an octagon-roofed tower with a finial at the rear, not incorporated into the roof but attached to the house. Like several of the significant early commercial buildings on

19. The Dominion Day, 1906, parade passing along East 3rd Street, showing 146, 152 and 154 East 3rd—the houses furthest to the left.
(Photographer unknown, NSMA 247)

lower Lonsdale, it was built by the Western Corporation.

One more curious building, at 123 East 3rd, attracts attention in the block east of Lonsdale: the Law Block, designed in 1913 for Vancouver Properties by the architect Alexander Law **(20)**. Like many other apartment buildings of the period, it has sets of finely crafted square bay windows on the front facade, but the building is unique because of its sloped roof—the architectural version of the snap-brim fedora. After several years of war, Depression, and little work in British Columbia, Law left for California in 1920, where the only fedoras were on Sam Spade.

Walk south on Lonsdale to 2nd Street.

Throughout the Lower Lonsdale area, the viability of the old buildings dating from North Vancouver's pioneer years is challenged by the new prosperity and the modern, metropolitan character of the offices and chic shops along the waterfront. In most cases, especially those of the buildings erected in the last ten years along the Esplanade, the juxtaposition of old and new—of the old wharves and new buildings at the Cates shipyard next to the Lonsdale Quay, for example—has worked well, and North Vancouver has done a good

20. The Law Block, at 123 East 3rd Street.

job of enhancing its historic flavour with devices such as the 1905 shoreline marker mentioned above.

From the corner of 2nd and Lonsdale, you can see one juxtaposition of the new against the old. At the northwest corner, with facades on both 2nd Street and Lonsdale, is the 1905 building originally owned by W.E. Thompson (who is possibly the builder and co-investor with Frederick Innes in the 1889 Innes-Thompson Building on Hastings Street in downtown Vancouver) **(21)**. With its copper dome, cutaway corner and corner entry, and finely detailed bays and two-storey facades, it is the epitome of the "friendly" town building that makes an essential contribution to the pedestrian nature of a major shopping street. To its west along 2nd Street *was* the 1911 St. Alice Hotel, a five-storey, brick-clad, reinforced concrete edifice that, even without its original cornice and with wrought-iron fire escapes tum-

21. The Thompson building at the northwest corner of 2nd and Lonsdale.

bling down its south and east facades, still managed to retain the sense of streetscape and homely, friendly, pedestrian orientation.

As land in the area was trading at such a premium, seismic upgrading of the St. Alice promised to incur substantial costs, and the existing city zoning promised great rewards to anyone erecting a new building, the old hotel became expendable and was demolished in the late 1980s amid a chorus of protest. The apartment building that replaced it is a stunning rapier of a tower, especially when viewed from the Lonsdale side; however, from the pedestrian's viewpoint, it becomes nothing but a horizontal building tipped onto one end. The

22. The Palace Hotel, about 1909.
(P. Timms photograph from *Vancouver Illustrated*, NSMA 5510)

streetscape for much of the distance formerly occupied by the St. Alice is now blank, devoid of the kind of architectural, retail or human interest that keeps pedestrians moving around on the streets.

The other old hotel that recently vanished from the Lower Lonsdale area is the Olympic, originally known as the Palace, at 140 East 2nd Street, a few steps to the east of Lonsdale **(22)**. Built in 1906 and, until 1915 when the second Hotel Vancouver opened, the only hotel in British Columbia with a roof garden, the hundred-room Palace was designed by Thomas Hooper who, with Rattenbury and Maclure, form the trio of great early architects in the province. The loss of these two hotels, the impending relocation or demolition of the Pybus cottage on East 1st, and the recent sale of the Syndicate Block at Lonsdale and Esplanade, indicate how fragile North Vancouver's heritage character has become in the superheated real-estate market of the 1990s.

Glossary

ARTS and CRAFTS STYLE. An outgrowth of the Arts and Crafts Movement in England, inspired by William Morris, C.F.A. Voysey and others in the late nineteenth century. Houses usually feature a sheltering, hipped roof; dormers also have hipped roofs; often there is half-timbering on the second storey. Arts and Crafts houses are fairly compact shapes compared with rambling Tudor Revival and Craftsman buildings. It is closely associated with the Craftsman style, but Craftsmans generally have gabled, rather than hipped, roofs, and have a lot more exposed structural elements. Arts and Crafts houses, regardless of their size, look as if they would belong in an English rural or village scene.

BALLOON FRAME. An economical house-building method that evolved about 1845 and, after about fifty years, began to be super-seded by the platform frame still in use today. A nailed-together skeleton of thin boards running the full height of the house formed the house's structural system (the balloon frame); floor joists and rafters were then attached to it. It replaced the costly, time-consuming, craft-oriented technique of notching and pegging that went into post-and-beam or half-timbered house frames, and thus helped to make possible the building boom of nineteenth-century North America.

BALUSTRADE. A series of balusters (posts between the newel posts of a staircase or porch railing) with a capping rail or coping.

BATTENS. Vertical wooden strips separating wall panels.

BELLCAST EAVES. A flared concave upwards shape built into the bottom edge of a roof surface, as in the shape of the lower portion of a bell.

BRACKET. A support between a vertical member (a post or a wall) and an overhang. In Carpenter Gothic architecture of the late nineteenth century, brackets were elaborately scroll-sawn; in the Stick style, brackets were straight pieces of wood set on a diagonal (with sometimes, in addition, another stick bisecting the right angle formed by the vertical post and horizontal overhang), as in rural Swiss cottages.

CALIFORNIA BUNGALOW. Small, boxy houses with low-pitched roofs, porches, and understated second storeys built between about 1910 and 1925. They were inspired by the so-called "Pasadena lifestyle," Japanese tea-house design, and the simple, garden-oriented, unfettered suburbia of southern California. In their use of materials and their reflection of a social aesthetic, they are part of the Craftsman style. The broad front porch evolved from the Cottage style—picturesque visions of traditional English houses as published in A.J. Downing's 1850 *The Architecture of Country Houses*. Many bungalows were built with a front stoop, rather than a full-width porch. (In addition to Craftsman influences, bungalow mania in North America was inspired by Spanish Colonial influences, Swiss chalets, the informal Shingle-style buildings of the eastern United States, and rural shacks and barns.)

CAPE COD STYLE. A breezy, informal house style inspired by the domestic architecture of the American eastern seaboard, and ideally featuring white-painted bevelled clapboard siding, shutters, wooden mullioned windows, and dormers set into a steeply pitched roof.

CAPITAL. The top elaborated part of a column, usually in one of the three classical orders derived from ancient Greek (Doric and Ionic) and Roman (Corinthian) architecture.

CARPENTER GOTHIC STYLE. Inspired by the Gothic Revival in England (the writings of John Ruskin and the design of the English Houses of Parliament), the invention of the balloon-frame method of house building and the steam-powered scroll saw for cutting wooden decoration, Carpenter Gothic was a popular architectural movement in North America in the last half of the nineteenth century. In addition to a profusion of decorative wooden fretwork (sometimes called gingerbread), Carpenter Gothic houses often had pointed windows like those of Gothic cathedrals, and asymmetrical, "organic" floor plans growing outwards from a central core, giving them a picturesque quality.

CHANCEL. The eastern part of a church, used by the clergy and separated from the nave by a screen or railing.

CLERESTORY. In church architecture, the upper part of the nave, choir and transepts above the roofs of the aisles, containing a series of windows that admit light to the central parts of the building. A clerestory can also exist in other types of large buildings, and were common in industrial architecture of the early part of this century.

CLINKERS. Bricks from the hottest part of a kiln, which have been overburnt and vitrified. They are usually extremely hard, dark in colour and often, having fused together in the firing, have to be broken apart, leaving jagged surfaces.

CORNICE. A horizontal projecting moulding crowning the top of a building.

CRAFTSMAN STYLE. Closely related to the Arts and Crafts style, and the most popular housing style in the Vancouver area between 1910 and 1925. Typical features are prominent, broad, gabled roofs, exposed brackets and rafter ends and, in the best examples, rough brick or stone for chimneys, foundations and porch piers. Siding is usually shingles, giving the buildings an overwhelmingly wooden look. The effect was a warm, livable building that was "natural" and true to its materials. The most famous Craftsman architects were Charles and Henry Greene of Pasadena.

DORMER. A vertical window with its own small roof and side walls projecting from a larger sloping roof.

DOUBLE-HUNG WINDOW. A window with two glazed sashes, both of which slide vertically within the window frame.

DUTCH COLONIAL REVIVAL STYLE. One of the period styles of the 1920s and 1930s, it revived features of American Dutch architecture of the eighteenth century, notably the gambrel roof. Another typical feature is a semicircular pediment above the front door.

EAVES. The projecting edge of a roof, which overhangs the side of a building.

EDWARDIAN BUILDER STYLE. See VANCOUVER BOX.

FINIAL. The ornamental finishing piece, usually spiky in general form, at the top of a spire, buttress, gable, or corner of a tower.

FRETWORK. Decorative woodwork, usually used as porch brackets or affixed to the fascia boards in the gable of a house, and sometimes called gingerbread.

GABLE. The triangular piece of wall beneath the end of a pitched roof.

GAMBREL ROOF. A dual-pitched peaked roof with a shallower slope above a steeper one.

GEORGIAN REVIVAL STYLE. A formal, symmetrical house type, built in Vancouver mainly during the 1920s and 1930s. Some of the larger and more elaborate versions have side gables and dormers. Most common are the hipped-roof examples such as those in Third Shaughnessy, which usually have stucco walls, restrained wooden ornamentation around the entranceways and windows, and a finely proportioned balance between windows and walls. The style originated about 1885 in the New York architectural firm of McKim, Mead and White, who were motivated by a desire to restore order and restraint to the architectural scene; many of their early houses featured wooden corner pilasters and Palladian windows. A builder's vernacular—described in this book as Edwardian Builder or Vancouver Box—grew out of that style and swept across North America in the years before 1910, at which time the Craftsman style went on the ascendant.

HALF-TIMBERING. In medieval times, a type of construction in which a large proportion of the building consisted of a heavy timber frame with the spaces between the framing members filled in with wattle and daub, brick or plaster; both the timber and the complementary material are visible. In the more recent era of balloon-framed and platform-framed wooden houses, half-timbering is a veneer, rather than the building's structure.

HIPPED ROOF. A roof that slopes on all sides from the peak towards the walls—changes in wall direction are accommodated by hips, not gables.

JULIET BALCONY. Any little balcony with a rounded balustrade, at which Juliet might have stood while declaiming ". . . wherefore art thou, Romeo?"

LOGGIA. An open-sided arcade.

NARTHEX. The vestibule stretching across the western (entry) end of churches, and separated from the nave.

NAVE. The body of a church, where the congregation sits.

NORMAN REVIVAL STYLE. In Vancouver, it was a period or revival style—appropriate to the nostalgic mood of home-buyers after the First World War—a few examples of which were built in the 1920s and 1930s. It started as a picturesque style in the United States in the 1880s, incorporating elements of traditional country houses in Normandy. Features included steep-pitched, conical or gambrel roofs, quoined corners, and round turrets—many of the same features that were part of the Richardsonian Romanesque style of the same period.

OGEE. A double continuous S-shaped curve that is concave below, turning into convex above.

ORIEL. A projecting alcove on an upper floor.

PALLADIAN WINDOW. Named after the sixteenth-century Italian architect Andrea Palladio, it was a design that was part of the Georgian style of architecture in England and the United States in the eighteenth century. It has three horizontal sashes, the middle of which is taller and semicircular above the tops of the outside two. Some "neo-Palladian" windows in developer-built houses of the 1980s and 1990s consist of three horizontal panes with a separate semicircular fanlight mounted above the middle pane; many of these houses also feature a large semicircular fanlight mounted above the front door.

PEAKED ROOF. A roof that slopes on two sides.

PEDIMENT. A triangular, partly circular or other geometric-shaped decoration crowning a window, doorway, archway, or other wall opening.

PILASTER. A column attached to a wall as though the column were half buried in the wall.

PLATFORM FRAME. The common house-building method of this century, in which the walls are constructed as ceiling-height panels, supporting platforms or floors; it was the successor to the balloon frame, in which floors were attached to a frame that extended the full height of the house. As it uses short lengths of timber as vertical structural elements (studs), platform framing does not require the high quality of lumber that was so readily available a century ago, and is no longer.

PURLIN. A roof member perpendicular to the rafters, and sometimes protruding underneath the eaves.

QUEEN ANNE STYLE. The culmination of all the Victorian-era house-building styles; it borrowed the asymmetrical "organic" house plan from the Gothic Revival, the fretwork from the Carpenter Gothic, the patterned surface texture of High Victorian Gothic and the half-timbering from the Stick style. Surfaces were textured or decorated, and steep rooflines often incorporated turrets—all for a picturesque effect.

QUOINS. Alternating large and small stones at a building's outside corners.

RAFTER. A roof member sloping from the peak to the wall.

SHED ROOF. A roof that slopes in only one direction.

SHINGLE STYLE. The shingle-covered country houses of the 1880s-era American eastern seaboard, emphasizing the strength, boldness and simplicity recalled from New England colonial architecture. It used design elements of the expensive, stone and masonry Richardsonian Romanesque style, but built them out of wood. Common elements include steep, curving rooflines, dormers, short towers, narrow eaves and wide, surrounding porches with shingle-covered posts.

SIDING. The weatherproof facing on the outside of a wooden building. The common materials of old Vancouver were sawn shingles, clapboard (bevelled boards laid horizontally with a slight overlap), shiplap (a narrower version of clapboard), and drop siding (wide boards laid horizontally with the thinner upper edge fitting beneath the "drop" of the board above—when seen end-on, a piece of drop siding has a "flattened S" profile). Later types of siding, either used in new construction or to modernize old buildings, include asphalt and asbestos shingles and "boards" of vinyl or aluminum. Stucco—a weatherproof plaster sometimes mixed with rock and glass particles and applied to a netting attached to the house's frame—became a popular finishing material in the 1920s. The brown "beer-bottle stucco" of the 1930s and 1940s is properly called Inisite.

SPANDREL. The filled-in panel between the head of a window and the sill of the one immediately above it.

SPANISH COLONIAL REVIVAL STYLE. Hearkening back to the buildings of Spanish California, the style features white stucco walls, round-topped windows, arches, tile roofs, and wrought-iron balconies, and began to appear in Vancouver in the late 1920s.

STICK STYLE. An outgrowth of A.J. Downing's cottage designs of the 1850s, the interest in Swiss rural architecture, and a desire for "truthfulness" in wooden construction, Stick-style buildings exposed the framing members of balloon-framed houses, and used diagonal braces for porch brackets, diagonal siding set within panels, and X-bracing, to create a stick-built look. Large, linear fretwork designs at the peak of a roof within the gable were also typical.

STREAMLINE MODERNE. The successor, usually seen in large commercial buildings of the 1930s, of Zigzag Moderne (which is often referred to as art deco). Streamline Moderne was an outgrowth of the machine aesthetic, and the fascination with the curved, streamlined forms of airplanes and automobiles. In buildings, characteristics are horizontal banded surfaces, rounded corners and parapets, the use of glass brick, and stucco siding.

TUDOR REVIVAL STYLE. The most popular period style in Vancouver in the 1920s and 1930s, reviving the picturesque architecture of Tudor England, including the half-timbering, steep-pitched gable roofs, diamond-mullioned leaded-glass windows, irregular floor plans and profiles, bellcast rooflines, black timbers interspersed with white plaster and, in the best examples, overgrown English landscaping surrounding the house. In the United States, these houses are often called Stockbroker Tudors.

VANCOUVER BOX. The style of builder's house, subject to infinite variation, erected throughout the city in the first decade of the century. Vancouver Boxes are relatively simple, symmetrical shapes; some were superb examples of craftsmanship, while others were poorly built with few amenities and little detailing. They often contain features of other styles, such as the Queen Anne and the

Craftsman, and were usually built by carpenters who took their cue from plan books that sired "builders' boxes" all over North America. The most common in Vancouver is the two-storey house with a front porch, a hipped roof and an oversized single "cyclops dormer"; in the United States, this particular design is considered to be an evolution of the Georgian Revival style.

VANCOUVER SPECIAL.   The most common speculative-builders' house since the mid-1950s. The classic "Special" is relentlessly rectangular, with a low-pitched tar-and-gravel roof, a brick-veneered lower storey, and a stucco upper storey with sliding glass doors opening onto a narrow balcony with a metal railing. Usually, the bedrooms are on the ground floor and the living area is upstairs; the ground floor is commonly at ground level, as the house is built on a concrete pad, avoiding the expense of excavating a basement.

Acknowledgements

W e want to acknowledge the assistance given to us by the following people:

The staffs of the Northwest History Room and Historic Photographs Section, Vancouver Public Library; the staff of the City of Vancouver Archives; Marco D'Agostini, Heritage Planning Assistant, City of Vancouver Planning Department; Nancy J. Kirk, for information on her grandfather, Edward Douglas, and the house at 5610 Angus Drive; Elinor Martin, who provided most of the information about the Miller family in Grandview; Margaret Walwyn, who provided copies of published material and archival documents about St. Mary's Church; Mrs. W.L. Warner, for information about her father, R.M. Matheson; Robin Fitzgerald, who helped research the Coffee Shop Tour on a summer job with the Community Arts Council and the Federal Government's Challenge 89/SEED Programs; Roger Neate and Ian Putnam, who enjoy walking as much as we do; Betty Skakum, for being patient and walking the routes and offering suggestions; Christine Allen, for whipping the manuscript into shape.

Bibliography

Allen Parker and Associates. *Vancouver Heritage Inventory, Summary Report*. B.C. Heritage Trust, 1986.

B.C. Mills, Timber and Trading Company. *Patented Ready-Made Houses*. Vancouver, 1905.

Ewert, Henry. *The Story of the B.C. Electric Railway*. Vancouver: Whitecap Books, 1986.

Foundation Group Designs. *The Ambitious City, City of North Vancouver Heritage Inventory*. North Vancouver, 1988.

Kalman, Harold. *Exploring Vancouver*. Vancouver: University of British Columbia Press, 1974.

Kluckner, Michael. *Paving Paradise*. Vancouver: Whitecap Books, 1991.

Kluckner, Michael. *Vancouver The Way It Was*. Vancouver: Whitecap Books, 1984.

Kluckner, Michael. *Vanishing Vancouver*. Vancouver: Whitecap Books, 1990.

Know Your City. Vancouver Civic Federation, 1925.

Morley, Alan. *Vancouver: From Milltown to Metropolis*. Vancouver: Mitchell Press, 1961.

Rushton, Gerald. *Whistle Up The Inlet: The Union Steamship Story*. Vancouver: J.J. Douglas, 1974.

Taylor, G.W. *Builders of British Columbia: An Industrial History*. Vancouver: Morriss Publishing, 1982.

Templeton Archivists' Club. *Vancouver: A Short History*. Vancouver: Templeton School, 1936.

The Fiftieth Anniversary—St. Mary's Church, Kerrisdale, 1961.

Vancouver Illustrated. Dominion Publishing Company, Vancouver, 1908.

Walker, Lester. *American Shelter*. Woodstock, New York: The Overlook Press, 1981.

Walwyn, Margaret and Spedding, Nan. *A Guide to St. Mary's Church, Kerrisdale*. Granville Deanery, Diocese of New Westminster, The Anglican Church of Canada, 1986.

Index

B

About the Authors

JOHN ATKIN has published a series of Vancouver walking tours for the Community Arts Council of Vancouver, in addition to his own *Interesting Objects* brochures. He has appeared on television and radio several times, undertaking a televised coffee-shop tour for U–TV in 1991.

Photo: Rosamund Norbury

MICHAEL KLUCKNER is an artist and writer renowned for his dedication to heritage architecture. He has authored several books on this subject, most recently *Paving Paradise*, winner of the 1992 Hallmark Society Award of Merit. He is president and founder of Heritage Vancouver.

Photo: Sarah Jane Allen